Beautiful Old Dogs

Beautiful Old Dogs

A Loving Tribute to Our Senior Best Friends

Edited by
DAVID TABATSKY

Photography by
GARRY GROSS

Foreword by
VICTORIA STILWELL

ST. MARTIN'S PRESS ♒ NEW YORK

www.stmartins.com

Design by James Sinclair

Library of Congress Cataloging-in-Publication Data TK

ISBN 978-1-250-03022-1

First Edition: November 2013

10 9 8 7 6 5 4 3 2

Contents

Foreword

Garry Gross was my business partner and my friend. Together, we formed Dog Trainers of New York, a highly successful, Manhattan-based dog training business that helped thousands of dogs enjoy better lives with their families.

Garry was a fabulous business partner whose energy and enthusiasm for the dog training profession was infectious. Both of us were dedicated to spreading the word about humane training methods and we would sit together for hours, talking about the cases we were working on, developing new ideas and comparing techniques. Although Garry was thirty years older than me our passion for dogs traversed any age gap.

When my idea for the television show, *It's Me or the Dog,* came to fruition, Garry was so proud of me. He was wonderfully selfless and supportive and made everyone who came into contact with him feel special.

Garry had turned to dog training after many decades as a top fashion photographer. Although he loved his second profession, the pull of photography never left him. Ten years after he began training dogs professionally, he decided to combine both his passions. The results were outstanding. Garry wanted to show the world how amazing dogs can be, and through the magic of his camera lens and his touch as a trainer every picture he took became a work of art.

Garry and I began working on a project we were very excited about. It was his aim to show the beauty and soul of every dog he photographed, but it was older dogs that fascinated him the most. Senior dogs are often the ones that get overlooked on the street or in a shelter, but Garry saw a lifetime of experience in their old and wizened faces.

All these dogs had a story to tell. The results, as you will see in this exquisite book, are nothing short of mesmerizing. Unfortunately, Garry is not here to realize his dream, but thanks to the wonderful David Tabatsky and Garry's sister, Linda Gross, the project has continued in his memory.

Garry, you made my life richer and I feel so fortunate to have known you. Thanks for all the great times we had and for all your support. You continue to live through this beautiful book, and the dream you had to celebrate the beauty and wisdom of senior dogs has now been realized.

Victoria Stilwell
Celebrity Dog Trainer and Behavior Expert
Author, TV Host, and Creator of *It's Me or the Dog*

Introduction

I didn't become a dog person until I encountered the exquisite photography of Garry Gross, specifically his soulful portraits of senior dogs. As an aging person myself (aren't we all), I was especially touched by Garry's concept of empathy—for aging dogs and humans, alike. *Beautiful Old Dogs* is the result, and I hope it's a fitting tribute to Garry's vision.

"The older the better," he said. "Dogs with soul in their eyes."

Garry's mission—to make the world a better place for both species—is not only admirable; it's an absolute necessity. Senior dogs deserve to be treated with the same respect and loving care that senior citizens of the human variety have the right to expect from society.

"Garry cared very much about all the dogs he photographed but he was especially passionate about senior dogs," says Leslie Jean-Bart, who assisted Garry in his photography studio in the heart of Greenwich Village in New York City until Garry died in 2010. "He saw a direct parallel between them and how senior citizens are treated. He often said that everyone loves to have a puppy, but no one cares about old dogs. He wanted people to see the beauty, dignity, and character of senior dogs so that they would become as excited about these dogs as they are about puppies."

But *Beautiful Old Dogs* is about more than compassion. It's meant to honor our senior best friends and explore their current state of care and custody, primarily in America but also in other countries and cultures that treat their elderly pets especially well.

How people regard *older* animals is especially revealing. Senior dogs are often overlooked, under loved, and mistreated; in fact, many are carelessly cast away to live out the last chapters of their lives alone, underfed, and in pain. Shelters usually consider senior dogs the least likely to be adopted, leaving them in the vulnerable position of being put down prematurely.

However, it doesn't have to be this way. There are more and more organizations devoting their resources to looking after senior dogs and attending to their plight, offering hopeful alternatives by finding aging dogs nurturing homes to live out their final years.

The reference guide at the end of this book—Resources for Care and Custody—offers practical information for those wishing to learn more about caring for senior dogs, both in their own homes and if and when they need outside help.

Gandhi once said, "The greatness of a nation and its moral progress can be judged by the way that its animals are treated."

With that sentiment in mind—along with Garry's mission—I hope this book will become a call to action, motivating readers to *do* something, whether it's adoption, rescue, or joining the senior dog bandwagon in whatever way possible. When more people become inspired by the unique qualities that senior dogs offer and realize how they can make their beloved pet's final years more comfortable, then the world will be a better place for us and our very special best friends.

Enjoy Garry's remarkable photography. Feel the heartwarming words. Then *do* something. Make a donation. Visit a shelter. Save a dog. Redeem yourself.

David Tabatsky
2013

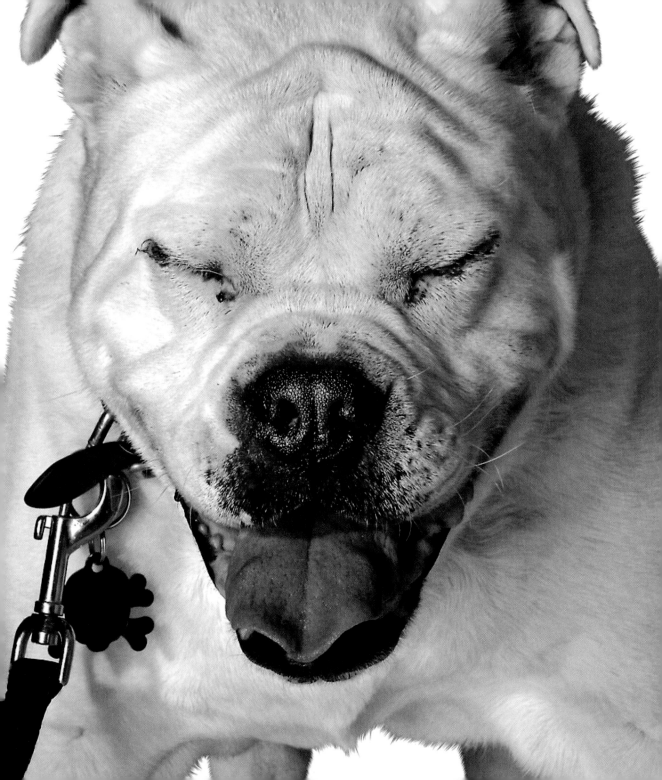

Beauty

This is the first photograph of a senior dog I ever did. As I looked through the lens of the camera, much to my surprise I was mesmerized. I saw wisdom. I saw his history. I saw the dog as a puppy running around. I saw some sadness. I saw so much beauty and that's what astounded me. Who ever thought about beautiful, older dogs? At that moment, my series of dog photos came to life.

Although for me, it goes beyond the project. I'm trying to make a statement here. It has something to do with the fact that this contradicts our natural understanding of what beauty should be. I think that we have to have a change of mind, a change of heart, a paradigm shift so that we can look at faces like these that are old and actually see the beauty of them; not just dogs but also humans.

These dogs are beautiful and they are also in need. These dogs have love and compassion and they are willing to give it to anybody who takes care of them. They're faithful and they're dedicated and it is my great hope that you will see the beauty in these senior dogs as deeply as I do.

Garry Gross
The National Arts Club
October 21, 2010

The Greatest Gift of All

To those of us who feel that dogs are one of God's most perfect creatures, we cherish every single moment with them in the autumn of their years. Oh sure, it's wonderful when they're puppies, romping and playing, tearing up newspapers and chewing on furniture. Then they bond with you and you learn that they are one of the few creatures in this world capable of giving unconditional love. No matter what happens, they always are there for you, through joy and sorrow, sickness and health, loneliness and despair. They are there, never judging. They take a place in your heart that is immoveable.

And when the years have taken their toll and they can no longer romp and play, they continue to give you all the love in their hearts. When they can barely walk, they look at you adoringly, seeking your guidance and help. We feel helpless at times and our eyes fill with tears as we try to comfort these precious babies. They deserve every bit of love and care that we can give, for they have given their all to us, for nothing more than a kind word, a gentle pat, or a kiss on the cheek.

When you look into their eyes, you see the soul of our creator. And as hard as it may be, when life becomes too difficult and the pain and suffering unbearable, we can give them the greatest gift of all, the peaceful journey into God's loving arms.

Doris Day

My Summer

by Trixie Koontz, Dog

Dad teaches me to type. Hold pencil in mouth and type. At first is fun. Then is not fun. He says to me, "Write, Trixie, write. Write essay for Web site." Being good dog, I write. Not fun, but I write. Expect treat for writing. Get no treat. Stop writing. Get treat. Carob biscuit. Good, good, good. Okay, so I write some more.

Dad promises Web site visitors my essay end of July. Must give up important ball chasing, important napping, important sniffing—all to write. Work hard. Writing hard. So many words. Stupid punctuation rules. Hate semicolons. Hate, hate, hate. Chew up many pencils in frustration.

Finish article. Give to Dad. Then I rip guts out of duck. Duck is not real. Is Booda duck, stuffed toy. I am gentle dog. Cannot hurt real duck or even cat. But am hell on stuffed toys. Work off tension. Rip, rip, rip. Feel pretty good. Cough up soggy wad of Booda-duck stuffing. Feel even better.

Dad gives editorial suggestions. Stupid suggestions.

Stupid, stupid, stupid! He is not editor, is writer. Like me, Trixie Koontz, who is dog. I pretend to listen.

Am actually thinking abut bacon. Bacon is good. Bacon is very good. I am good, too. People call me "good dog, good, very good." Bacon is very good. I am very good. But I am not bacon. Why not? Mysterious.

Then I think about cats. What is *wrong* with them? Who do they think they are? What do they *want*? Who *invented* them, anyway? Not *God,* surely. Maybe *Satan?* So nervous writing about cats, I use too many italics. Then I hit hateful semicolon key; don't know why; but I do it again; and whimper.

Dogs are not born to write essays. Maybe fiction. Maybe poetry. Not essays. Maybe advertising copy.

Here is my advertising copy: BACON IS VERY GOOD. BUY BACON. BUY LOTS OF BACON. GIVE TO ME. THANK YOU.

Dad gives me editorial notes for study. Eight pages. I pee on them. He gets message.

Dad says will give my essay to webmaster as is. Webmaster is nice person, nice. She will know good writing when she sees it.

Days pass. Weeks. Chase ball. Chase rabbits. Chase butterfly. Chase

Frisbee. Begin to notice sameness in leisure-time activities. Pull tug-toy snake. Pull, pull, pull. Pull tug-toy bone. Pull, pull, pull tug-toy rope. Lick forepaw. Lick other forepaw. Lick a more private place. Still do not taste like bacon. Get belly rub from Mom. Get belly rub from Dad. Mom. Dad. Mom. Dad. Get belly rub from Linda. Get belly rub from Elaine. From housekeeper Elisa. Belly rub, belly rub. Read *Bleak House* by Mr. Charles Dickens, study brilliant characterizations, ponder tragedy of human condition. New tennis ball. Chase, chase, chase! Suddenly is September.

Webmaster asks where is Trixie essay? Where? Dad lost. Dad got busy working on new book, got busy, forgot fabulous Trixie essay, and lost it. My human ate my homework. Sort of.

All my hard work, my struggle, so many hateful semicolons. All for what? All for nothing. Essay lost. All for nothing. Feel like a character in *Bleak House*.

Think about getting an attorney. Get literary agent instead. Writing fiction. Novel. Maybe knock Dad off bestseller list. Teach him lesson. Writing novel called "My Bacon" by Trixie Koontz, Dog. Already have invitation from Larry King, David Letterman, be on shows, do publicity, sell book, get belly rub from Dave. Maybe get limo for media tour. Ride around in limo, chasing cats. Life is good when you're a dog.

Dean Koontz

The Virtues of Older Dogs

At Cocker Spaniel Adoption Center, we are frequently called to rescue older dogs, and we often find ourselves with a large number of "senior citizens," some more senior than others. Many people tell us they are not interested in adopting senior dogs precisely because they are older.

We find these attitudes senseless and unacceptable. There are so many virtues in older dogs. They are typically gentle and easy going, and most of the time they cause no trouble in their homes. This makes their frequent abandonment all the more painful.

Most rescuers I know prefer to have older dogs in their foster homes. I cannot tell you how often I have heard: "They are my favorites." I share this viewpoint entirely. Older dogs are so special and dear. To know them is to fall completely in love. If only more people would give them a chance.

Most people want puppies. This is not always a good thing for the puppies. In many cases, people don't realize what they are getting into when they get a puppy, and when they find out how much work a puppy takes, many wish they had adopted an older dog that is comparatively easy to care for.

If you adopt an older dog, you would be giving him a precious chance to have the life he truly deserves. It is certainly not their fault that they have aged. It happens to everyone. It's true that some older dogs will need special care as they enter their golden years. So will we all—one day. Some of us are there already.

Think about how you would want—and need—to be treated when your step slows, your vision isn't as clear, your hearing not as keen, your memory not as sharp. If you fall sick, wouldn't you want loving hands to hold and hearts to care? No one knows how many breaths are left in any of our bodies, so we need to live for today, and let our animal companions do the same. Give an old dog a chance.

Valerie Macys, Ph.D.
Cocker Spaniel Adoption Center, Inc.
Elkridge, Maryland

A Special Touch

My big brother Garry had a way with animals. Lost dogs followed him home like nobody else. Garry's fascination with animals and wild life brought a wide variety of temporary boarders into our midst, including tropical fish, turtles, frogs, salamanders, chameleons, mice, gerbils, white rats, a rabbit, parakeets, a parrot, numerous cats and dogs, a ring-tailed monkey, and homing pigeons.

He and his friends built a pigeon coop in a small vacant lot adjacent to the driveway at the back of our house. Starting off with two or three pairs, they mated the birds and helped raise their young until they had a medium-sized flock. The birds were all patiently trained to return home, first from short and then increasingly longer distances. Everyone marveled when a bird with a "secret" message wired to its leg would be thrown up into the air, circle to get its bearings, and then zoom off across the sky. A confirmation phone call occasioned each successful delivery. The bird returned to Garry's coop several hours later, or perhaps the next day, with a "secret" response we all eagerly awaited.

But Garry had a special thing for dogs. When we lived in Mount Vernon, New York, our neighbor's German Shepherd accompanied him daily to the school bus stop, waited for the bus to arrive, watched until the vehicle was out of sight, and then trotted home. Come three p.m., he was back at the designated spot, patiently awaiting Garry's return. Garry knew nothing about training dogs back then; he was only eight or nine years old, but he already displayed a special connection with animals.

Many years later, when Garry came to the end of a successful career as an advertising photographer, his life-long love of dogs ignited a new endeavor—Dog Trainers of New York, which flourished in short order. Beyond his acquired professional qualifications, it was Garry's natural affinity for dogs that inspired his success. It was as if he were a boy again—charming, sensitive, and genuine, always ready with a funny story, making friends easily and inspiring confidence. These days, when I consider the course of his too-short life, I can only marvel at the person he became, not by chance but by choice.

Linda Gross

Be Gentle: I Know My Dog Is Old

A Call for Improving Etiquette with Older Dogs

Like everyone else in society, loudly lamenting a decline in civility, I recognize there are new breaches of etiquette every minute. Like cell phones. But there is one type of impolite behavior among adult humans that goes pretty much unchecked. I've been guilty of it myself.

I am referring to the blunt, utterly uncensored and often just plain mean things people say to us about our dogs (by "us" I mean dog people). My close friend Pam has a twelve-year-old German Shepherd who is visibly aging. So are the rest of us, human and canine, but to what person would you ever be so crude as to say, "Is that your mother? Wow, she looks awful. She can hardly move!" Yet this is the unsolicited blubbering my friend endures from strangers, all day long, about her old dog. I empathize because I've been through this three times, beginning with our family Beagle, Sam, who lived to be nearly seventeen, mostly out of spite.

"How old is he?" People would ask this unrelentingly about my now-departed Irish setter, Amos. I didn't mind telling them that he was twelve or thirteen. "Wow. They don't live much longer than that, do they?" How tacky is this?

But it gets worse.

When my big, hairy mutt, Louie (we called him our "Bavarian crotch smeller"), was old and frail, someone once asked me, "Have you thought about putting him down?" First of all, that's kind of like asking a woman in her forties (this also happened to me), "Have you ever thought about having children?" "Gee, there's an idea! Why didn't I think of that?" When your dog is old and sick, the end is pretty much all you can think about. Your heart is breaking and you're preparing yourself to come to that decision in a way that spares your dog unnecessary suffering while giving yourself time to feel as peaceful as possible about letting him go.

People assume they can say anything they like about a stranger's dog.

Pam is at the point where she dreads walking her dog in public because she knows passersby will make insensitive comments she can't bear to hear. Out in the world she is thoughtful and tender enough not to remind everyone she encounters that they are mortal. Like the rest of us, she can tell when a person's on his or her last legs, but she keeps herself from saying, "Gee, you sure are slowing down" or asking the person's daughter, "So how long do people in your family tend to live?"

When approaching people like my friend, it helps to remind oneself that she knows her dog is old. She knows it every waking second of every day.

The last years and months we share with our geriatric dogs are among the most bittersweet times in a dog lover's life. We know, from the moment we choose these guys as puppies or meet their limpid stares at the animal shelter, that our hearts will be torn apart some day. What makes it so much worse is that the older they get, the sweeter they get, and when they reach absolute critical sweetness—when you simply cannot love them any more than you already do—they grow completely exhausted and die.

So when you see a person patiently coaxing an old dog on his increasingly shrinking route you are witnessing someone who could benefit from a little compassionate restraint. Consider a simple hello for the owner or a tender pat on the head for the doggie emeritus. Like most of our mothers told us at some point: if you don't have something nice to say . . .

Susan Seligson

My Fountain of Youth

This may sound strange, but it's true: Old dogs taught me how to stay young in body, mind, and—most important—spirit.

What's the definition of "old" anyway? Veterinary medical research has confirmed many times over what dog lovers already knew, that dogs age faster than we humans do. We used to calculate a dog's age in human years with the times-seven formula. But recent studies reveal that the first year of a dog's life is equal to about fifteen human years, not seven. So beautiful old dogs are even more superannuated than previously suspected! Which means there's even more to appreciate and look forward to.

Dogs may age faster than humans, but they do so with infinitely more grace. When people age gracefully, they're acting like dogs in the best possible way. Dogs age well because they don't think about life; they're too busy enjoying it. What's more, they don't label themselves "old."

That said, cruel people know how to make a young dog old before his time. Abused dogs age faster than properly pampered ones. But love is such powerful medicine that even small doses work wonders on prematurely aged dogs. And in heaping helpings, the antioxidant love works at the cellular level to energize the entire physical body via the soul. Loved dogs, liked loved persons, display a puppy's eager resilience even if they've gone gray about the muzzle.

I ought to know: After several protracted separations from my husband of seventeen years, and many doomed attempts at reconciliation, our divorce was finalized, and I reentered the dating scene at age forty-four. People in my neighborhood who'd seen me carry the invisible weight of that unhappy marriage suddenly saw a happier, younger woman, and told me as much.

At forty-six, I gave online dating a try; at forty-seven, I fell in love. I never looked better in my life, not even in my twenties.

Of course, the other key to reversing the clock is daily exercise. For dog lovers, this one's a no-brainer—with a dog, you walk, and that's the heart-healthiest exercise there is, for both of you.

At age thirteen, my Border Collie Sheba shrugged off severe arthritis and seduced a much younger male dog named Piggy, who remained my furry girlfriend's devoted, saucer-eyed suitor for the rest of her life. That same year, Tiki, my thirteen-year-old Chow-Rottweiler cross, bravely fought oral cancer, and won! Dogs can battle cancer with astonishing results because they don't accept the dreaded disease as "a death sentence" the way many people sadly do.

I've rescued many dogs over the years. Several were already up there in age when they arrived, like sweet Sasha, the thirteen-year-old Maltese. To make this dog more "adoptable"—because, sadly, many adopters are ageist, rendering beautiful old dogs in shelters the last to be adopted and first to be killed for cage space—I got to work polishing her inner puppy.

To help ease my dogs' aging pains, I give them wholesome food in strict portions and supplement their diet with Omega-3 oil for joint health, plus virgin coconut oil for brain health, milk thistle to reverse ocular cloudiness, hawthorn to strengthen the heart, anti-inflammatory cinnamon and turmeric, and probiotics for immune support. I bathe them in chemical-free shampoo made with organic Neem oil, a super-emollient biopesticide.

After just a few week of this therapy, Sasha's inner pup came out to play. This little-old-lady dog looked so youthful, no one could believe she wasn't a youngster!

I became determined that all the dogs in my care would stick around as long as possible. And then I realized that, if I wasn't careful, my dogs might outlive me, and then who'd fix their dinner with such attention to detail? That's when the dog's aging pains became my aging gains. I adopted the K9 health regimen I'd designed for them, with very positive results. And when I stabilized my health and ran out of fixer-upper foster dogs, I applied my life-extension techniques to my human loved ones. Now, whenever folks in my circle face a health challenge, they call me for advice—and they call me "Doc."

But the real natural-born life-extension experts are the beautiful old dogs; the ones overlooked at animal shelters across this country and around the world; the ones tragically, erroneously dismissed as "past their prime." They instinctively know how to stay youthful. Thanks to them, I've located the fabled fountain of youth. And so can you: It's any place on earth you find a beautiful old dog.

Julia Szabo

The Big Blue Elephant

I didn't write this. My dog did.

I shuffled around some of the words. I filled in some of the gaps to match my recollection of the truth, and, in doing so, repaired some of the great liberties he freely took with history, I suspect at my expense. I also labored a bit over the intended meaning in each of the scribblings I found on small scraps of white, lined paper over a period of time, lying underneath the blue satin feet of the Big Blue Elephant—a five-foot-tall stuffed animal postured aside the blue velvet rocking chair where my wife and newborn son, William Dylan, spend most of each day and much of the quiet hours of the night locked in the intimate embrace of nursing. If you were to shift your gaze from Madonna and son down to the base of the chair and onto the deep blue rug, you would see my very white, fifteen-and-a-half-year-old Maltese, Scoshi, spying from deep within the folds of an also-white, fluffy shag blanket, which he has raked into position— never twice the same—with his front paws.

Scoshi seems to feel perfectly camouflaged here for his recent, self-appointed mission to guard the infant feeding post. From his low perch on the floor, he could easily fire off a few barks across the bow at anyone, even me, who might enter little William's all-too-blue room. The quick hail of barking, however, would eventually give way to a fit of sneezing and snorting as his allergies kicked in. The volatile mix of barking and sneezing would then knock him off balance and he'd fall on his rear end. He'd give himself a quick, arthritic shake—his work clearly done—rake the white shag blanket back into position, lie down, and ready himself for the next attack, or possibly a nap.

From this strategic point, however, Scoshi could also keep one eye trained on the Big Blue Elephant as it cast its very broad, very blue shadow over both mother and child, just inches away. While the Big Blue Elephant had been silent and still for the eight weeks since little William first came home from the hospital, apparently its tranquility and its soft, shimmering baby blue fur and black button eyes were fooling no one, least of all Scoshi. He knew that a Big Blue Elephant must clearly be respected for the danger it represents. If the Elephant made one sudden move toward the feeding chair, it would be go-time.

Over the eight weeks of this silent, blue vigil, however, gravity was beginning to take a toll on the Big Blue Elephant, causing it to slump slowly into an almost impossible yoga pose with its trunk buried deep between its fluffy blue legs (no, don't try this). So, one crisp winter afternoon, early in the new year, I picked up the Elephant, readjusted its stuffing, and attempted to return it to regal form.

As I lifted the blue carcass, that's when I found it—a small scrap of white paper under the left foot of the Big Blue Elephant.

I picked up the piece, unfolded it, and read the words, while my mind stood still from the wonder. There were just two lines on a torn strip. That was all.

> *Dear Little Pink Thing,*
> *Who are you?*

From the simple substance of the note, the author was abundantly clear to me. And it was equally clear that this note was not meant for me, but for someone else. It was written by Scoshi, and meant for my firstborn son, who lay in the arms of my wife, just a few feet away.

I put the note back at first, a bit embarrassed and ill at ease, as though I had just become an uninvited diary reader, peeking at pages that I should not. But as the weeks passed, I went back time and again. I was as curious about the intent as I was the content.

It was not the last note I would find. Over the next several months, more would appear. Some were longer and more developed, the paper unevenly folded. Gradually they became a small stack that lay beneath the Elephant's foot—I always put them back after reading—and they were beginning to upset their already fragile blue ballast.

I'm not sure when it was that the meaning behind the whole litany of messages began to become clear to me in a larger sense. It couldn't have been more than a few weeks after a few more notes made their way under the Big Blue Elephant.

I was certain of this: These were not random notes. They were secret notes. They were the type of notes that would be passed by hand, from schoolboy to schoolboy to schoolgirl on those halcyon days that boys discovered that girls were no longer *icky*. They were crucial notes—the kind quickly scribbled to a loved one and entrusted from soldier to soldier at the point of no return. They were sacred, final notes that old men write to their children, their wives, and their God that sometimes go undelivered.

These were notes on manhood. They were life lessons from a wise old dog to a little boy who would barely know him.

There is a painful paradox in the overwhelming joy of welcoming little William to our family, and that is that he will probably never have a chance to know the little dog who sits below him so loyally like the Keeper of the Gates. At nearly sixteen, Scoshi has the experience of more than a century of dog years mixed with the crusty, deliberate spirit of a drill sergeant. But his little black button eyes are heavy now. He can no longer hear. He moves slowly with a limp. If he stands too long in one place, his legs slide out from under him. He waits quietly and patiently at the foot of the stairs now, hoping that someone will come along and remember to carry him up. Watching life leave slowly is sometimes unbearable.

Of the many dogs that have crossed the path of my life, Scoshi has been my closest companion. Wherever I would go, he would go. We traveled across the country together. We have shared glasses of wine from the tip of my finger. We have fished together some of the simplest and most unyielding waters of the world. He has run and trained with me for marathons. He has walked many beaches with me, at sunrise and sunset, in celebration and in sadness.

Ultimately, these memories will be only mine, though, not shared by my son. William will go on to play fetch with someone else. Another dog will lick his face. It stings me to contemplate that and hurts even worse to put it into words on a page. But I know that it will come to pass.

Perhaps that is why Scoshi wrote this: to leave a sort of silent legacy behind. Perhaps it is not enough for him to be the constant guard at the foot of the chair—these little notes are Scoshi's synthesis of life, a crude and simple compass for William, for when Scoshi is no longer there to lay at his feet.

Perhaps, too, these notes were meant for me to discover. I find it so strangely coincidental that these brief little epistles were found, of all places, under the foot of the blue beast that was the cause of Scoshi's constant watch. It was as though he knew that I would eventually find them, as though he wanted me to. In much the same way that a criminal mind will unconsciously turn itself in, the contemplative mind will always find a way to communicate its deepest truths. I think Scoshi meant for me to reflect on them with my son. These were lessons for us both to ponder.

In my own defense, however, I would have eventually gotten around to writing something of substance to Will. Scoshi just beat me to it. No doubt the timing was intentional, too. While I have no proof, I suspect that he simply didn't trust my ability to sufficiently convey the lessons of manhood to my firstborn son on my own. I imagine he wanted first crack at it. After all, there lies at the heart of every grown male a deep desire for the chance to explain the world to a little boy.

Perhaps that is why Scoshi wrote this. His thoughts seem succinct and to the point. Along with his natural distrust in my ability to handle the subject of manhood, he probably senses in me the resurrected spirit of my Uncle Cal, a long-winded Don Quixote and self-ordained poet who can successfully obscure the simplest of truths by buckling you over in boredom.

Ultimately—I will never know why, exactly—he reached out to little William (and to myself, perhaps). I know many things about dogs. I know that their love and their loyalty are blessed with permanence. I know that when they wag their tail, it is connected to their heart. But there are many things I do not know about dogs, not the least of which is what they like to ponder and then write about.

So, if you can believe that you can find new purpose with the birth of a child; if you can believe that the world is full of Big Blue Elephants that sit quietly, seductively, yet ominously nearby, no matter how blue or safe our surroundings; if you can believe that the lessons of life that protect us are never really new, that they are learned through dog years of experience and then shared with the young who follow; if you can believe in the love of a little old dog for a little boy who will never really know him ...

Then you can believe that I didn't write this. My dog did.

John O' Hurley

Garry's Passion

Garry cared very much about all the dogs he photographed but he was especially passionate about the senior dog project. He saw a direct parallel between those dogs and how senior human citizens are treated. He often said that everyone is always excited about puppies and loves to have one, but no one cares about the old dogs.

I assisted Garry in his studio as a way to overcome my fear of certain types of dogs. During the early shoots, it was very important to Garry that the dogs look straight into the lens. He thought it was the only way to let the viewer peer into their "soul."

Since the eyesight of senior dogs as well as their hearing were more often than not seriously impaired or completely nonexistent, we often had to go to great lengths to capture their attention and get their eyes to focus into the camera. I would stomp the floor with force, slapping it as hard as I could while Garry, perched on a ladder a floor below to be at eye level with the subject, would make all sorts of dog, cat, and human sounds, often to no avail. That is, until that fleeting second when the dog would gaze directly and intensely into the lens.

Whenever we completed a shoot, we would always comment on how tough it was, which was quickly followed by Garry saying, "But we have not lost one yet!"

But over time, as Garry photographed more and more senior dogs, he started warming up to the idea that the posture of the dog and the location of its gaze can be as telling and as powerful as when they stare directly into the lens. Accepting this approach gave us much more flexibility and the sessions became an even deeper time of bonding with the animals.

Ultimately, Garry wanted to make people see the beauty, dignity, and character of these senior dogs. He wanted all of us to be as excited about these dogs as we are about puppies.

Leslie Jean-Bart

Old Dog's Dream

A long run, then a leap over the chicken-wire fence.
He rolls in the dirt between the lettuce rows,
barking, jumping puppy-wild, and the rabbits scatter
like pigeons before a motorcycle, dashing through
their shallow tunnels and into the woods.

He sits back on his hind legs, licks a paw, lord of all,
until he hears his name and scampers for the driveway.
"Hey, boy," and up into the passenger seat he goes,
paws draped out the window, head craned to the wind
that crazes his fur, eyes shut tight. It is his bliss.

Then he wakes, curled in the oval bed, his paws
cradling his ashy snout, stiff legs pulled up
beneath him. The television is on, so he limps
to the couch and his master helps him up into
his place beside, pats his flank, scratches his ears.

He settles in, rests his head across
the old man's thigh. His tail flicks once.
But his rheumy eyes shine, and in his mind he is chasing rabbits,
and the highway wind still whistles past.

Richard Storm

My Mentor

When I first showed up at Garry's doorstep, searching for a dog trainer apprenticeship, I didn't have a clue what I was in for or who Garry Gross was, either. First, he gave me the cold shoulder, saying he didn't mind an apprentice. Yet he allowed me to sit at his clear plastic table with the funny chairs and asked me what use I could be. As I rambled on about horses and dogs, Garry began warming up. But he still had no use for an apprentice, or so I thought, until I noticed a little glint in his eye. I knew he was having fun with me, pushing me, toying with me to see what I would say while bringing out my drive to work with dogs.

Garry could do that. He could look at you and wager how much fun he could have with what you had to offer. Fortunately for him, as I would later learn, he had such friendly eyes that you could never hold it against him. Garry was one of the most confident people I'd ever met. I kept coming by for months just to show him how eager I was to learn from him because I was sure he was the best dog trainer in the city. The walls of Garry's studio, covered with pictures of all the dogs he had trained, attested to that.

But Garry was already past his prime time as a dog trainer, which he'd been doing for over ten years. He explained that the work was always the same, with small variations, that he had his fun and the learning curve had ebbed.

I think Garry kept me around until he realized that my true value was my potential to take over his dog training company so he could follow his true passion—photographing senior dogs. Garry was obsessed about dogs growing old.

"Have you ever seen a really old dog?" he asked me. "They can look right through you. They know who they are, what they like and dislike, and if they are willing to get up to say hello to you."

I learned from Garry that a dog's personality is it's strongest trait and is something to be admired. This is what you can see when you strip away their leashes and take a portrait. This is what Garry saw. The subjects were mostly deaf and blind and had no teeth. Getting them still and focused in the frame was hard enough, but Garry always captured a shot that all of us loved. The biggest payoff was creating a permanent image for the owner of their lifelong friend. Fortunately, most of these images can now be shared with all of you.

Jessica Jacobson

Chasing Waves

Doug the Dog is completely deaf, partially blind, and has taken to standing in front of a random wall and licking it. He is often befuddled yet dignified in his seventeenth year. He has an old man aroma—slightly stale, rotten toothed, and damp from the growths that sprout like mushrooms on his hind legs. We have been told we should get another dog so the transition between now and what is to come will be easier.

"We are dog people," I remind my husband, when he declares Doug our last pet.

Nobody told me that getting a dog when your kids were little would mean the kids and the dog would age out at the same time. I don't know how it has come to this: having an empty nest and old dog named after my kids' favorite cartoon character of the time. Just when we are finally free of the joy of teenagers, we have to contend with the guilt of leaving behind a confused and slightly daft dog.

We adjust to changes. Doug can't go to the Pet Hotel anymore because he's an old bag of bones and won't eat or drink when we leave him. Which is why he was at the New Year's Eve wedding of our oldest daughter this year. She wanted to be married at the same beach where Doug once chased waves, back in his younger years, barking furiously at their crest and crash, determined to beat back Mother Ocean's relentlessly tormenting tricks.

"He's not too bright," commented a spectator back then, watching the futile, frantic sprints of a young, spry Doug the Dog as he raced up and down the shoreline, hoarse with the fury and responsibility of his mission.

Of course, I was offended, enough that I still remember it now, so many years later. That man only saw a dog's ridiculous effort to catch a wave, but I saw the pursuit of potential and the sweet thrill of possibility.

But I must admit, other than treeing squirrels, Doug has never had too many other talents to speak of. He is loving and loyal but not the brightest crayon in the box.

When our last daughter left for college, Doug waited every afternoon next to the front door for her to return. Nothing we did could dissuade him from his vigil. One night, a few weeks after she left, I heard the pitter-patter of his toenails tapping into our bedroom. He stood at the edge of the bed and looked up at us, his eyes filled with sorrow. I patted the mattress on my side, and he jumped up, barely, walked in circles, twirling the blanket into a nest, let out a long and mournful sigh, and went to sleep.

He sleeps with us now, even when the girls return. I think he knows better than to let his heart get broken all over again. I admire him for that.

Maybe someday we'll get back to the beach.

Carolyn Mason

A Man and His Dog

MAN: You were always a lot of trouble.

DOG: *Thanks a lot. You think I'm a grumpy old dog.*

MAN: When you were a puppy, you shredded everything you could get your paws on.

DOG: *And what do I have to thank you for?*

MAN: You cost me a ton of money to replace the things you destroyed, and then to replace the things I replaced that you also destroyed.

DOG: *You never gave me chocolate.*

MAN: True.

DOG: *Or onions or garlic or avocado or alcohol or coffee or tea or grapes or raisins or milk or other dairy products or macadamia nuts or candy or gum or bacon or persimmons—*

MAN: And your point is?

DOG: *Or peaches or plums or raw eggs or raw meat or raw fish or salty food or sugary food or sugary drinks or yeast dough or raw potatoes.*

MAN: That's quite a list.

DOG: *Phew!*

MAN: You took up a lot of my time and effort raising you and training you.

DOG: *Did I mention chocolates?*

MAN: Now that you're an old dog, you sure cost me a ton of money in veterinary bills.

DOG: *Did I leave anything out? You sure did. You left everything out.*

MAN: You eat up a lot of my time tending to you even when you're relatively well and even more when I have to nurse you when you're sick, which is more often now.

DOG: *Once in a while, but not often enough in my opinion, you do give me well-cooked lean meat and slices of apple and orange and banana and watermelon (after removing the seeds, of course) and carrot and green beans and cucumber and zucchini and a plain baked potato and boiled white rice or pasta.*

MAN: You will always be a lot of trouble.

DOG: *And plain boiled chicken. Ooh. That's always good.*

MAN: And you're worth every bit of it.

DOG: *Thanks. Thanks a lot. Thanks man.*

MAN: Don't mention it.

DOG: *So what am I supposed to do now? Lick your feet?*

Anonymous

Nala: R.I.P., 1999–2012

In the fall of 2010, my best friend Nala and I were both diagnosed with cancer.

Nala, a splendid Rhodesian Ridgeback I had been taking care of for several years by virtue of owning a pet sitting company, had cancerous tumors in her hind leg. After extensive surgery, she healed slowly but completely. My surgeries and chemotherapy left me severely worn out.

As we recovered over many months, Nala and I did not see each other. I looked at her photo every day and the thought of seeing her again got me through an arduous journey back to health.

I remembered the first time I met Nala, after she arrived here in New York from Texas. I was immediately taken by her size and how regally she carried herself.

As an animal-care professional, I have minded all kinds of animals, especially dogs. But in all the years I've spent committed to this work, I have never developed a relationship with one particular creature as I did with Nala.

Little did I know how much she would teach me about loyalty and unconditional love.

Soon after, we begin our walking schedule. Nala wasn't especially impressed with me, maybe because she was so upset with her new home. She charged at me from the next room, barking with the typical attack.

"I'm sorry you're so unhappy here but if you let me, we can have fun," I said to her, staring right into her eyes. "What do you say?"

Nala sat down, let me put her leash on, and our friendship began. She greeted me each day for the next seven plus years with her tail wagging as she nuzzled her head into my body.

During all those years, Nala consistently tried new things with enthusiasm and curiosity, never with anxiety or reluctance. She lived every minute fully.

Nala was a born athlete, focused and muscular. She competed in lure coursing for years in Texas and I loved watching her compete in New York. She played to win but also had fun.

She didn't have a mean bone in her body. When I brought Nala to doggy day care, everyone admired her as she methodically searched the room for scent. She taught the younger dogs how to slow down and focus.

When we finally saw each other after our long separation, it was a joyous reunion. Nala did not want to rest or be restricted in her activities while I could barely move. Still, we were thrilled to be together again.

I brought her a stuffed animal, which she always loved. She excitedly tore off the wrapper and ran around with the squeaking toy. Her reaction always made me smile and feel like I was watching a child opening his or her first meaningful birthday present.

Nala always showed a similar enthusiasm and appreciation for the simplest of gifts. Her behavior taught me to follow my instincts and live each day with joy and simplicity.

Less than two years after facing cancer, Nala was unexpectedly diagnosed with acute renal failure. The ensuing months of medical treatments were an emotional roller coaster. Nala remained regal, calm, and courageous. She never complained. In her last weeks, we showered her with steak, pizza, burgers, and anything she wanted. We knew when she stopped eating that she was getting ready to leave us. In her last hours, her tail wagged and she made her usual circle before lying down.

I lost my best friend today.

Barbara Napoli

The Elder

The other day, I took my lanky, fifteen-year-old Flavio out to a local café, where, over the course of the afternoon, about two hundred people loved on him—lumbering giants, baby talkers, drug addicts, homeless people, caffeine-charged students, grabby toddlers—he didn't care, he was like Tony Bennett out there, smiling and holding court with dog lovers who knew how special he was, how rare and fleeting. They fed him an onion bagel with cream cheese, some rips of jerky, latte foam, and around twenty dog cookies. And I let them.

But he tired of the treats and accolades and attention after a while, and gave me that look, as if to say "this is flattering and all, but Dad, I need to grab some carpet and take a nap." So I took him home and he slept solid, had a running dream, and didn't wake up until evening kibble hit dog dish. Not so deaf yet, this one.

Flavio is so calm now, so anchored. He won't run off, even if the side gate or front door is left open. He doesn't have accidents unless he's sick, destroys nothing but food, and can be left in the house for hours without concern. A Shepherd-Chow mix, he's patient and kind with adults and kids, and loves all dogs, even when they don't love him. Though he still makes an effort to catch squirrels, he knows it's just for pride's sake now, and that going through the motions shows me that he still cares.

As we get older, we develop habits. I incessantly crack my right big toe, mumble to myself, watch too much television, snore, clear my throat like an old lion. I make wine, and garden like my grandfather did. I complain that kids and dogs these days have no discipline or purpose. I'm a curmudgeon: a mostly affable one, I hope.

That's what happens to old dogs. They get easy, and, well, a bit eccentric. Old dogs grunt, groan, and snore, and get odd growths, worn brown teeth, and bare spots. They eat more slowly, and treat the food bowl like it's a portal of godly wisdom. Old dogs stare out the window or at you, and carefully plan the ascent of steps instead of leaping up them. They dream more—about squirrels, maybe, or of beady-eyed, nasty raccoons in the backyard at night. Elder dogs lose their hearing, but it happens so slowly they almost don't seem to suffer or mind, their rituals are so ingrained. Maybe they welcome the quiet.

Flavio incessantly licks at the carpeting in the family room. I think he likes the feel of it on his tongue. Or maybe it's just what he does to help pass the time, like knitting, or crosswords.

He has "backward sneeze" jags every other week, and goes through bouts of chewing on his butt, for absolutely no reason. No fleas, no dermatitis, no dirt. He simply likes it, the same way my eighty-eight-year-old dad likes to rub the crown of his head over and over while he thinks too much about the Yankees or the Mega Millions lottery.

Flavio smacks his lips at night, over and over, as if reminiscing over the evening meal. He labors over just when to lie down and when to get up, because at his age, it's no easy deal to get that lanky bulk to rise or fall. He has taken to lying right in front of the door to the family room, even though he knows someone is bound to open it right into his face at any moment. He's begun to savor holding a rubber ball gently in his mouth, like a guppy holding its young.

He sighs, he reflects. I'm not sure why I believe this, but I suspect he's thinking about his dear departed dog friend Lou a bit more these days. I can feel it in him.

It's peaceful, and stately, this time with him. It's the calm before the storm, I know, but right now, I'll savor Flavio's deliberateness, his bearing, his eccentricities. It comforts me, and helps evoke thoughts of dogs long gone, especially Lou, my last elder to pass, a dog who was as good and brave as any dog who ever lived, who saved Flavio's life, and mine, twice. It makes sense then, my thought that Flavio must think of Lou from time to time, especially now that he, too, is old, and close.

At each birthday for the past five years, Flavio has gotten a birthday "meat cake," replete with peanut butter frosting and the appropriate number of candles, which, for some reason, he has not yet learned to blow out. And as time marches on and he gets slower and more gristled, I find myself taking more and more photos and videos of him, almost as a father might of his young child, for memory's sake, for posterity. Funny how I never thought of taking many photos of him when he was a young, fast, handsome escape artist. We dog owners seem to do things in reverse, at least when it comes to love, and remembrance.

One day, perhaps Flavio's six year-old brother Rico will become an elder statesman, too, learn introspection and restraint, and become a model for some young upstart. When hell freezes over, no doubt. But today, I'll enjoy Flavio, and I'll make sure he knows I do.

Steve Duno

Tiloc

Oh no, this is one ugly dog, I thought, taking a look at Tiloc, lying on the backseat floorboard of my friend's car. Since her parents were moving and couldn't take her with them, I had volunteered to find Tiloc a new home. We met at a park to make the introduction, and as soon as Tiloc got out of the car and ran through the trees she suddenly transformed into this beautiful, black-and-white, exotic girl. Then she sat on my feet. Oh no, game over. This dog wasn't going anywhere.

That was thirteen years ago.

Tiloc was just a pup when I adopted her. She had a gorgeous, slick black coat, with undertones of brown and four symmetrically white speckled paws. She also had a white-tipped, foxlike tail that I would call her "bicycle flag." She wasn't big on cuddling, but she was fiercely loyal from the start and definitely preferred being with me than anywhere else.

Since I grew up with Cocker Spaniels as our family pets, it was exciting and challenging to have an Australian Cattle Dog mix as the first pet of my own. But it became clear fairly quickly that I was out of my league. Tiloc was smart and needed way more stimulation than I could provide while living in an apartment in the middle of Los Angeles. So, I did what any other dog-loving fanatic would do. I turned my life totally and completely upside down to accommodate her.

Tiloc doesn't like kids, crowds, or many other dogs. She's been attacked at dog parks and she's done her own fair share of attacking back. We've moved three times. She's driven cross-country with me and accompanied me to New York, Georgia, Kentucky, Texas, Canada, and all over California. She's learned to herd sheep and come to understand more than forty vocabulary words. She could have learned even more if I wasn't so busy balancing being a single pet parent with the rest of my life.

I've often felt guilty about Tiloc, worried that I wasn't providing her the best life possible. Sometimes I've stressed over her mental wellbeing more than my own. Since she was so fast, independent, and highly intelligent, I regularly struggled with the idea of finding her yet another home, one better suited for such a capable dog.

Finally, a friend said to me, "Elaine, *you* are where Tiloc needs to be." Smart friend.

Now, Tiloc is almost entirely gray. I watch her move from rug to rug like she's island-hopping, magnetized to the places where she can stand without sliding. She's survived cancer surgery and is covered with lumps that may be fat or tumors; there are too many to count and at this point, she is too old to worry about them anymore. Managing Tiloc's pain and keeping her comfortable is my top priority. She is riddled with arthritis and clicks when she walks. She stays mostly to herself in the middle bedroom, which has become her cave. She'll have bursts of energy, but her final days are nearing. Nothing can deny that.

Between daily medications, injections, and weekly massages, I'm still turning my life upside down for this dog—and I wouldn't have it any other way. No matter where I go, what I do, or who else I may bring into my life, Tiloc holds a special place in my heart. She was my first baby and had a roster of nicknames to show for it: TT, T-poo, Googie, Baby Girl, Princess, Boo Boo, Goose, and Tiloc Hendrix.

But she will forever be "My Original Girl."

Elaine Hendrix

Binkie's Gift

By the time my grandfather reached his eighties, he seemed resigned to rotting away all by himself. I'd often find him sitting half dead in a rocking chair, alone, as if he was just waiting for his life to end. Since my grandmother had passed away a few years before, Gramps let himself go. At first, he stopped gardening and soon enough he wasn't eating the fresh food that had kept him healthy for so long. And he wasn't moving around anymore. Instead, he favored that old rocking chair and his couch in front of the television. It wasn't long before his health was failing and his spirit was at an all-time low.

That's when Binkie, a splendid Boston Terrier who must have been at least eight or nine years old, came into the picture and gave Gramps a new lease on life. It was as if my grandfather had been waiting for his new companion all his life. In what seemed like no time at all, my eighty-eight-year old grandfather who had never cooked a complete meal in his life, went from rotting away with a remote in his hand to happily preparing home-cooked meals twice a day for his beloved Binkie. Not only that; Gramps started eating better, too.

And they walked together for miles every day, slowly but surely, deep into the woods behind Gramps' house. It wasn't very long before his blood pressure decreased and his heart rate slowed and with that, his attitude reversed and he became stronger and actually began smiling again. If I hadn't witnessed all of this with my own eyes I would have never believed it were possible. Binkie transformed my cranky, miserable old grandfather into the loveliest man you could ever meet.

I've learned to never underestimate the power a dog can have over a senior citizen. A dog can raise his spirits like nothing else I could've imagined. A dog can get even the loneliest person out walking in the sunshine and busy in the kitchen, adding a bounce in their step and a renewed purpose to their life.

Gramps lived on to ninety-seven, walking and cooking every single day for that little dog.

Dogs and seniors. A miracle combination.

Anonymous

Gar & Mar

Garry and I met forty-seven years ago, when we were graduate students at the University of Connecticut, in a town called Storrs in the middle of nowhere. We were probably the only New Yorkers in the entire graduate school and definitely the only Jews. I called him Gar. He called me Mar.

We immediately became best friends, bonding together with our "borrowed dog," an old Beagle we named Mansfield who lived next door to Garry's off-campus house and always stopped by after our nightly dinner together to play with us and eat our cookies.

When Garry told me he'd decided to become a photographer I was dumbfounded. It was such a huge leap from his major in speech pathology. But with his unwavering commitment and natural talent, I knew that Garry would succeed. And he did. My father, who owned an advertising agency specializing in fashion, hired him to shoot many award-winning ads.

Garry and I remained close throughout our lives. I knew all his girlfriends and he knew all my husbands. Garry was the most special friend in the world: kind, loyal, and generous. He was always so enthusiastic about his new projects, like a teenager getting his first car. I can still picture the merry twinkle in his eyes and that easy laugh, like a child's giggle.

I have always admired Garry's courage. Just as he unexpectedly became a photographer, Garry reinvented himself as a successful dog trainer and then a brilliant photographer of dogs. Just a couple of years ago, I joined Garry at the National Arts Club in Manhattan, where the audience loved his touching comments about inspiring people to adopt aging, homeless pets, kind of like Garry and I had done many years ago, with our old and hungry friend, Mansfield.

As I watched Garry share his remarkable photographs that night, it was clear that he'd created a very special body of work. I am thrilled that the world is now getting to see these exquisite images.

Mara Kurtz

Sky

I was certainly warned. I did my best to prepare. I read recommended books and articles about the looming "empty nest syndrome," about the radical shift in daily structure, about the phrases to use to ease the mental and emotional transition, about the small repetitive actions to take that can calm that immediate startling state of aloneness.

And yet, a heaviness and sense of loss permeate every room. There's an aimless wandering about, a lack of interest in heretofore attractive—even wonderful—distractions, a seeming refusal to engage with the suddenly unfamiliar environment in the apartment. I've noticed a tendency to compulsively walk in and out of Rebecca's room and an inability to resist the pull of her rumpled still fragrant bed. I've become afraid that once ensconced in her sheets, the body will simply dissolve there, never again moving even an inch away from what's left of her physical presence.

She's in college. It had to happen. It was explained. And yet I cannot snap the dog out of it. He's depressed. I don't need to anthropomorphize anything here. I recognize the signs of depression when I see them: a loss of appetite, a tendency to sleep all the time, a sharply decreased enthusiasm for venturing outside unless absolutely necessary. Oh no, I recognize this. The Greyhound is way down.

And I am, selfishly, a bit glad. I don't have to feel crazy about sighing frequently, or about picking up random objects and simply staring at them or about having Rebecca's T-shirt folded under my pillow. I am not alone in this. I have a partner now.

When Sky was rescued from the racetrack and Rebecca and I drove up to Albany to meet him, I was witness to the perfect match. Both long-legged, both gentle-spirited, they took off in a kind of skip and jump onto a wooded trail and then disappeared for an hour. I stood with Paula, intrepid and courageous Greyhound rescuer, and learned about Sky's life. He'd spent it in a crate and on the track. He'd raced in Florida and Arizona.

Like other Greyhounds, he'd received electric shocks as part of his training; he'd never known a friendly human, he'd never lived inside, he didn't know about steps, windows, mirrors, elevators, safety, or warm beds. He'd been treated like a fast machine designed to run well, take rough treatment, and make money, inevitably to be replaced when he stopped performing well.

But Paula also told me that even after all of it, even after that kind of life, "they still hadn't broken his spirit." And she was right. He was perfect for Rebecca. They slept together every night. They played. She taught him to trust. He'd curl up and make strange Greyhound sounds while she worked on her laptop or Skyped. He followed her everywhere and was always at the front door waiting for her when she came home. He only went there for her. He seemed to know when he heard the elevator arrive if it would mean Rebecca. Through those painful and often lonely middle school years, he was her anchor. I was often at a loss, but the dog seemed to intuit how to navigate. Sometimes, it seems, the best thing to do is follow at a respectful distance, find a discreet spot close by, and then quietly lie down.

And Rebecca gave that racetrack throwaway a world that is a safe and comfortable and simply wondrous place. She gave him quite entirely his life.

So, you see, I understand his devastation. I understand his loss. We're both waiting at the door now. And even though we're sure she'll be home soon, with new smells, and a new laugh, and a contagious excitement for what her new life can offer, we can't help but feel a bit robbed. Because we can't follow her where she's going now. Not this time.

So we take walks and share some meals, and while away entire evenings watching MSNBC. We make the attempt, but we know. Things will never be the same again. And our world, though certainly still safe and comfortable, is now somewhat less of that simply wondrous place.

Ally Sheedy

Lucky

I hope you get the honor of caring for a senior soul.

Every morning, when I wake up and see my sweet old boy laying next to me,
his stomach slowly rising up and down with each breath, I can be thankful
for another day of his love—for his sloppy kisses, for feeling his soft velvety fur,
for cuddling on the couch, for seeing his tail wag, for having my shadow for another day.

I wouldn't trade every extra sloppy kiss, hug, or moment of cuddle time
for a better decorated house or fewer loads of laundry.

I hope you get the honor of caring for a senior soul.
It is a roller-coaster ride many days, with moments of happiness,
fear and gratefulness randomly taking over.

I know how fortunate I am to still share my life with Lucky.
These wonderful moments will forever be etched in my memories.
while the minor inconveniences will long be forgotten.

Tanya and Toby Tobias
Second Life, * Avondale Estates, Georgia

*Second Life is an upscale thrift store in the Atlanta, Georgia, area that was created with the mission of giving homeless pets a second chance at life.

The Last Will and Testament of an Extremely Distinguished Dog

This is the full-length version of Eugene O'Neill's classic piece, which he wrote to console his wife, Carlotta, shortly before the death of their dog, Blemie, from the illnesses of old age.

Last Will and Testament

I, Silverdene Emblem O'Neill (familiarly known to my family, friends, and acquaintances as Blemie), because the burden of my years is heavy upon me, and I realize the end of my life is near, do hereby bury my last will and testament in the mind of my Master. He will not know it is there until I am dead. Then, remembering me in his loneliness, he will suddenly know of this testament, and I ask him then to inscribe it as a memorial to me.

I have little in the way of material things to leave. Dogs are wiser than men. They do not set great store upon things. They do not waste their time hoarding property. They do not ruin their sleep worrying about objects they have, and to obtain the objects they have not. There is nothing of value I have to bequeath except my love and my faith. These I leave to those who have loved me, to my Master and Mistress, who I know will mourn me most, to Freeman who has been so good to me, to Cyn and Roy and Willie and Naomi and—but if I should list all those who have loved me it would force my Master to write a book. Perhaps it is in vain of me to boast when I am so near death, which returns all beasts and vanities to dust, but I have always been an extremely lovable dog.

I ask my Master and Mistress to remember me always, but not to grieve for me too long. In my life I have tried to be a comfort to them in time of sorrow, and a reason for added joy in their happiness. It is painful for me to think that even in death I should cause them pain. Let them remember that while no dog has ever had a happier life (and this I owe to their love and care for me), now that I have grown blind and deaf and lame, and even my sense of smell fails me so that a rabbit could be right under my nose and I might not know, my pride has sunk to a sick, bewildered humiliation. I feel life is taunting me with having over lingered my welcome. It is time I said good-bye, before I become too sick a burden on myself and on those who love me.

It will be sorrow to leave them, but not a sorrow to die. Dogs do not fear death as men do. We accept it as part of life, not as something alien and terrible, which destroys life. What may come after death, who knows? I would like to believe with those of my fellow Dalmatians who are devout Mohammedans, that there is a Paradise where one is always young and full-bladdered; here all the day one dillies and dallies with an amorous multitude of houris, beautifully spotted; where jackrabbits that run fast but not too fast (like the houris) are as the sands of the desert; where each blissful hour is mealtime; where in long evenings there are a million fireplaces with logs forever burning and one curls oneself up and blinks into the flames and nods and dreams, remembering the old brave days on earth, and the love of one's Master and Mistress.

I am afraid this is too much for even such a dog as I am to expect. But peace, at least, is certain. Peace and long rest for weary old heart and head and limbs, and eternal sleeps in the earth I have loved so well. Perhaps, after all, this is best.

One last request I earnestly make. I have heard my Mistress say, "When Blemie dies we must never have another dog. I love him so much I could never love another one." Now I would ask her, for love of me, to have another. It would be a poor tribute to my memory never to have a dog again. What I would not like to feel is that, having once had me in the family, now she cannot live without a dog! I have never had a narrow jealous spirit. I have always held that most dogs are good (and one cat, the black one I have permitted to share the living-room rug during the evenings, whose affection I have tolerated in a kindly spirit, and in rare sentimental moods, even reciprocated a trifle). Some dogs, of course, are better than others. Dalmatians, naturally, as everyone knows, are best.

So I suggest a Dalmatian as my successor. He can hardly be as well bred, or as well mannered or as distinguished and handsome as I was in my prime. My Master and Mistress must not ask the impossible. But he will do his best, I am sure, and even his inevitable defects will help by comparison to keep my memory green. To him I bequeath my collar and leash and my overcoat and raincoat, made to order in 1929 at Hermès in Paris. He can never wear them with the distinction I did, walking around the Place Vendôme, or later along Park Avenue, all eyes fixed on me in admiration; but again I am sure he will do his utmost not to appear a mere gauche provincial dog. Here on the ranch, he may prove himself quite worthy of comparison, in some respects. He will, I presume, come closer to jackrabbits than I have been able to in recent years. And, for all his faults, I hereby wish him the happiness I know will be his in my old home.

One last word of farewell, Dear Master and Mistress. Whenever you visit my grave, say to yourselves with regret but also with happiness in your hearts at the remembrance of my long happy life with you: "Here lies one who loved us and whom we loved." No matter how deep my sleep I shall hear you, and not all the power of death can keep my spirit from wagging a grateful tail.

Eugene O'Neil

Wisdom

Scout, a sweetheart of a black Lab from the end of the block, was out for her usual morning stroll in the neighborhood, slowly accompanying her human on their daily trip to the local bodega for coffee and a newspaper.

Her human is my friend Bern. He's a big-time attorney, but on the street in the early morning hours he's just another dog guy in a hat and T-shirt with a plastic bag, doing his morning routine. Like many of us in our Upper East Side neighborhood here in New York City, he is known more for his dog and consequently is "Scout's dad" to a lot of folks.

Here, if you're out walking your dog (or dogs), you just come to expect that any greeting goes first to the dog—"Hey, Scout!" After that, you might get an acknowledgment, perhaps something less enthusiastic than the greeting that your dog got. And, even though people are quick to know your dog, they might not know your name—you'll often have to settle for a nod and "How ya doin'?"

Those of us with dogs will tell you that our dogs define the neighborhood culture and social scene. The dogs are the great equalizers, bringing people together every day. It often starts with the very simple request: "May I pet your dog?" There is no phrase that brings together people any better than that one does. Diplomats should all get dogs and get to work making friends with each other.

My wife, Cheri, and I joke that we might not know anyone in our neighborhood if we didn't have dogs. Instead, we have a rich collection of friends and acquaintances: doormen, parking attendants, food vendors, street characters, nurses and doctors and other medical professionals heading to work at the nearby hospitals, people with their earbuds in, people in business suits, people in T-shirts, people hauling their children around, people just hanging out.

At the age of thirteen, Scout was slowing down, and her one-block journey each morning was becoming more and more labored. Nevertheless, Bern faithfully and patiently allowed Scout this daily ritual, no doubt knowing how much it must have meant to her to have the time with him. My guess was that for Bern, it wasn't about the coffee—it was a combination of his sense of duty and his love for Scout. It was wonderful to witness this two-way devotion every morning.

When you have a dog, whether or not you are smart enough to realize it, this faithfulness and patience in the daily routine from start to finish is part of the deal. So in spite of the fact that we were watching Scout nearing the end of her life, we could all smile at what we got to see every day. I know that Bern would have done anything for Scout, and Scout would have done anything for Bern. She may not have done it as quickly as she would have in the past, but she would have done it.

One morning, watching Bern head back up the street with Scout, I said to him, "I guess you don't have many early morning appointments at the office these days."

He paused, looked at Scout, and smiled. She kept trudging along, not wanting to slow her momentum. She knew that he would catch up.

"You know," he said, "Scout has taught me that you don't need to go through life in a hurry. You see so much more when you go slow."

Ah, wisdom. Bern's a smart guy; he gets it. But as good an attorney as he might be, I bet he rarely says anything this powerful in any courtroom. I am never surprised by the simple eloquence that dogs inspire from their people.

Scout passed shortly after this, and all of us in the neighborhood mourned the loss of a family member. It doesn't take Bern as long to get to the bodega every morning now, but I'm sure that Scout is still making that trip with him every day. And even better, he left him with a piece of wisdom that may not be taught in law school, or in any school, for that matter.

In my world of dogs shows and training, we always worry so much about what we teach our dogs—to stand, to move, to heel, to sit, to behave—and that's a good thing. But as we saw with Scout, what's far more important is that we learn from our dogs.

So pay attention.

David Frei
The Voice of the Westminster Kennel Club

A Certain Genius

Garry and I were first cousins, born six months apart, but I really only knew him for the past fifteen years, until his death in November 2010 when he had just turned seventy-three.

We met by chance one evening, after hardly seeing each other for decades and never having really talked. That random night began a string of several years of almost weekly dates, full of intense, funny, and astonishingly honest conversation. We usually got together at his place, usually in the company of a dog, and we would talk for hours.

Garry and I shared family and many similar life issues: being single, teaching, and ersatz Buddhism. We cherished our evenings, graced with music, dogs, photography, and whiskey.

The openness and fearlessness of our talks brought an unexpected intimacy into our lives. We talked about Garry's fear of being alone in his old age and my expectation of it. I was in a state of comfortable denial but for Garry, growing old and the prospect of growing really old was deeply troubling. But Garry, like all artists, surmounted his angst by turning it into art.

A certain genius must have been involved in his evolution: first, the extraordinary career change from fashion photography to dog training. And then, the aching recognition of his own aging that helped him see the tragic nobility of the old dogs he began photographing, so different from the fashion models to whom he had dedicated his eye, artistry, and libido for so many years.

Garry's beautiful work in this book is the culmination and triumph of his life and art. And if he didn't think so, I would argue with him well into the night.

Beverly Gross

Dog of a Lifetime

The family room was the bustling hub of our home. It housed the big comfy sofa, TV, toys, computer, piano, and a separate basket for the dogs' toys. My two children and three large dogs congregated there, each of them busy doing their thing. As I worked at the desk facing the window, I often wished I'd had eyes in the back of my head. Little did I know that Rocket, our adorable Shepherd puppy, would one day make that wish come true.

From the beginning, Rocket was an exceptional pup. Unlike our others, he never went through the normal destructive teething phase. He knew which toys were his and *never* picked up anything that wasn't. Rocket was careful even then, and we remarked at how unique he was.

German Shepherds are working dogs, and if given a job, live more balanced and fulfilling lives. I was a busy mother, and keeping everyone fulfilled was important, yet not always possible. Genni, our Golden Retriever, stayed balanced by retrieving tennis balls and assorted items around the house. Anna, our female Shepherd, liked canine agility and we took classes together. Rocket, our youngest, did not have a job so he created his own career, brilliantly taking on the role of canine police officer! He kept a keen eye on the other members of his pack. "Observe and report" was his motto. Rocket would notify me when anything was amiss, thus becoming "the eyes in the back of my head."

Silly human that I am, I did not understand at first what he was communicating. Rocket's reporting method involved whining and nudging my hand—either off the keyboard, piano, or kitchen table.

"Do you want to go out?" I'd say.

No. That wasn't it. Is he asking for petting? No. That wasn't it, either.

Before long, I learned Rocket was reporting to me that something was wrong with one of his fellow canines. He would whine and nudge me to report that Genni was chewing her bandaged paw or obsessively licking the floor. He would let me know that Anna was in the act of shredding the carpet pad or jumping up on the kitchen counter.

"Ahh Ahh," I would shout to the other dog, interrupting their mischief, and tell Rocket "Goood little tattletale" while patting his head. In fact, Rocket became so good at his job that he would notify me if another dog was about to vomit! Over the years, Rocket saved me from many a gooey mess.

A few years had passed when we received devastating news that our fourteen-year-old son Matthew had been diagnosed with Ewing's sarcoma, an aggressive and very rare bone cancer. Prior to him undergoing a below-the-knee amputation, Matthew expressed a wish to take Rocket sheepherding. He always wanted to know what Rocket would do if he were freely turned out with sheep. We arranged a herding lesson to find out.

Rocket did not disappoint. He entered the ring with the handler and instinct immediately kicked in. Rocket zipped out, running circles around the sheep. He ran after a stray and finished by assisting the handler in pushing them into the pen. It was as if he had done it all his life.

What a gift for Matthew!

Our family beamed with pride as Rocket jumped into the water trough where the dogs go to cool off after work. The handler told us that Rocket had more talent than many Border Collies she trains.

Fast-forward a few years. At the end of a valiant fight, cancer had taken our son. All three dogs were home with us as Matthew took his last breath; each member of our family grieving intensely and each dog reacting to the loss in their own way. Our sensitive Shepherd, Anna, always crept out of the room when I began to cry. Genni kept up her happy Retriever demeanor. Rocket was strong and always ready to sit by our side or hold still so we could cry into his fur.

With the passing of a few more years, Anna and Genni, both old and beautiful dogs, have left us. Our daughter is off to college. We have entered the "empty nest" phase with Rocket by our side. He is now a distinguished senior at age eleven. His ears have turned from black to silvery gray. He is a bit stiff and doesn't hear as sharply, yet he intuitively knows that his only job now is to love and be loved.

Rocket's presence has been constant through the best and worst times of our lives.

He is our dog of a lifetime.

Ellisa Levant Beaver

A Cycle of Love

There is a cycle of love and death that shapes the lives of those who choose to travel in the company of animals. It is a cycle unlike any other. To those who have never lived through its turnings or walked its rocky path, our willingness to give our hearts with full knowledge that they will be broken seems incomprehensible. Only we know how small a price we pay for what we receive; our grief, no matter how powerful it may be, is an insufficient measure of the joy we have been given.

Suzanne Clothier

Chasing Fire Engines

I'm nuts about dogs. People often look like their dogs. I wish they'd act like them, too. Dogs are generous animals. You run into the odd crazy one, but dogs are so kind, so courteous. They are loving and loyal, and we could all use friends like that. They will tolerate things that bore them to death, just so they won't hurt your feelings. They're nice that way.

Dogs never forget how to play. Old dogs have as much fun as puppies. They're up for everything. They have the curiosity of a child, and they never lose it. They are always high. Lucky dogs.

I AM crazy about dogs. I admire them enormously. Noble beasts, always saving people's lives, pulling them out of rivers, scaring off thugs, finding lost kids. They are our oldest friends.

Dogs will die for us. Better yet, they will live with us, and it's much more fun with a dog around. I know why we like them, but why do they like us?

Sometimes they're our only friend. There's no ugly to a dog. They allow us to take care of them, and they take care of us. They make us laugh. They're good for our health, our heart, our liver. Some work in nursing homes and hospitals. Dogs don't care about wrinkles; they don't judge or criticize, they make you feel loved and needed, no matter how young or old or screwed-up you are. Dogs are good for you.

And they're fun. They don't sit around bitching about nothing to do. They are always up for adventure. Sometimes people jog with their dogs. I wish I were a dog; I'd chase joggers, the sweaty ones in their underwear. But city dogs have to be leashed, so they don't get much running in. It's like you only see fat lions in the zoo. Some dogs get to run in the park and I love watching them play. They know their parole is a short one so they get in all the fun they can. It's nice watching innocence, even if it is a dog. No beach is complete without one.

I have always loved and admired dogs for their dogginess, because they ARE dogs. I never saw them as little furry people. They are nothing like people, they are like dogs, a nicer species. I love watching them, playing with them, knowing them. I wish I were more like a dog, but I'm working on it. I was probably a dog in another life. Maybe that's why I chase fire engines.

Jill Freedman

Dancing with My Four-Legged Partner

Dancing has never been my forte. In fact I'm a lousy dancer and that's a shame because I love the exhilaration of being swept across the dance floor to the beat of some contagious song.

Ten years ago, dancing took on an entirely new meaning when the Guide Dog Foundation for the Blind in Smithtown, New York, matched me up with a fifteen-month-old Lab Poodle cross named Mark, who won me over immediately. But we didn't become an instant team. Grabbing onto that harness handle and stepping out into the real world with my life in Mark's paws required a gigantic leap of faith, much like what I imagined sky diving must feel like the first time you propel yourself out of a plane at God knows how many feet. So when Mark took off like a Ferrari on our very first walk together during training, forcing me to hold on for dear life, let's just say I felt somewhat unsettled. To make matters worse, Mark seemed more interested in sniffing the ground, picking up discarded food from the street, and chasing kids on skateboards than he was in doing his job guiding me.

"Trust your dog," the trainers said over and over.

Mark and I came home from training to the Upper West Side of New York City where we had to contend with a new working relationship on our own. We all have this image of a guide dog who simply obeys commands, and lies discretely under a piece of furniture when his handler is in conversation with other people, but Mark didn't match this robotic stereotype. He was simply a dog with a job thrust upon him that he happened to be good at. The stubbornness and smarts of a Poodle combined with a Lab's playful nature often caused Mark to question the status quo by refusing to respond to a "sit" or to "stay" only for a few seconds before running to someone to be petted. Friends and colleagues shook their heads, wondering if having Mark as a guide dog was a grave mistake. However, slowly but surely, Mark began to prove himself worthy of the job.

One day three months later, Mark and I were walking home from a rehearsal. I was in my second year of my master's at the Yale School of Music, and New Haven was aglow with a crisp autumn sun, and the trademark New England fragrances of fall. Dazed by the exuberance of this amazing season, Mark and I found ourselves almost gliding, as though borne on the wind itself, back to my dorm. Suddenly, I was struck by the most incredible revelation. This was the very first time I had experienced a carefree walk with Mark. Not once did I have to scold him for snarfing something off the street or turn his attention to his job. Mark was leading me effortlessly, turning left and right without hesitation until we were at the large gate in front of my dorm. Mark and I were finally experiencing the one thing guide dog handlers live for, like a mother hearing her baby saying "Mommy" for the first time. We had actually become a team. Even better, it occurred to me during that unforgettable walk that for the very first time in my life, I had been dancing. Mark's strong Lab-like pull, and his graceful Poodle turns made it feel as though my guide dog was a skilled leader in a winning ballroom dance team, and once I let go of my own inhibitions and hang-ups, I merely had to succumb to his movements and follow him. If I succeeded in doing so and Mark could feel my trust through the harness handle, that dance, scored by the music of the wind, traffic, birds, and choruses of people talking and laughing, would become the dance of my liberation and independence.

Mark became an extension of me, a creature with whom I shared a telepathic connection. Eventually, I stopped having to tell Mark where we were going. He seemed to know instinctively, or by listening to conversations between me and my partner Jenny before astounding me and taking me automatically to the door of the market I wanted to go to, even when he was used to going to another market on that very same block. He seemed to know when I was running late to one appointment or another, walking even faster than his normal brisk gait.

Nature is cruel as it relegates humans and dogs to such different life spans, taking away these wonderful creatures we humans come to rely so much on just when the working relationship becomes near perfect. I retired Mark just two months before his ninth birthday, leaving him to make a graceful transition into retired life with my mother in California. Shortly thereafter I was back at the Guide Dog Foundation, meeting a young, black standard Poodle, named Popeye.

On my first trip back to L.A., Jenny and I decided to take our dogs on a walk. Jenny was holding Mark's leash and Popeye was walking with me in harness as my guide. When we opened the front door, Mark would not take one step out into the fresh air. This was not the Mark I knew, the one who would practically pull me over like a child, urging his mother closer to an amusement park. No matter how much we coaxed, Mark would not budge. Then it came to me. Mark had never walked with anyone else when I was around. Sure enough, as soon as Mark was at my left side just like old times, he snorted happily, and began to lead the way. His ability to guide hadn't deteriorated either, as one might think. If anything, it had gotten even more refined, as though he was trying to say, "See what you gave up when you retired me?"

Mark's skill and experience made me lament the fact that youth can be wasted on the young, and that it was a true senior dog whose wisdom and experience I longed for. But at the same time, I had to acknowledge that Mark was a senior dog and I had to say good-bye. As soon as Mark saw our suitcases he took refuge on the opposite side of the house so he didn't have to watch us leave. It's the same thing every time we visit. Walking out that door without him is like being forced to sever a cord that has connected us over and over again.

Mark will never be old. His hair gets grayer, but that's been happening since he was five. Even as he ages and gets sick, he will never really leave me. There's no such thing as a world without him.

Being a good dancer requires not overthinking things and being spontaneous with your body without worrying about what people think. A dancer simply dances. That's how Mark goes through life. He never misses a beat. He takes every new situation as it comes, and steps gracefully into it, no matter what changes or pain he faces. I know Mark will continue to age in the same way.

Just as I suddenly learned to trust him as he navigated me around bus stops, parked cars, and crowded subways, I need to follow his example of entering new chapters in life. People ask me all the time if it's hard to switch roles from being the recipient of Mark's services to playing the role of caregiver. Mark and I have always had a give and take relationship. He guided me, and I fed him and took him to the vet. He gave me freedom and I gave him security. The older Mark gets, the more I value each moment with him. I've heard from many a guide dog handler that no matter how many wonderful guide dogs you have, there is always one that is particularly special. Mark will always be that dog for me, as he was the one who taught me how to dance.

Laurie Rubin

Best First Boyfriend

Garry's family agreed to let him have his first dog when he was fifteen years old. He knew that he wanted a German Shepherd puppy so one Sunday the family drove from the Bronx to a kennel where he could choose one. I was fourteen and his first girlfriend, and I had always longed for a dog. Garry invited me to go with him to find a puppy. He chose a beautiful dog named Elmo who he immediately loved, but on the trip home he put the puppy in my lap to show me it was also mine. Garry knew how much it would mean to me. He was the most caring, thoughtful, best first boyfriend any girl could have. Of course, we remained good friends forever.

My heart aches, as I write this, with gratitude for his love and generosity when I needed it so much. I always loved Garry. He was my teenage life.

Ann Prival

Ready for Love Again

You can get really close to a Yorkshire Terrier because you can take them just about anywhere.

For nine years, my Yorkie came with me wherever I went—to the theater, the studio, on airplanes, and in hotels. In restaurants, I kept him inside my bag and no one even knew he was there. He was my secret pal. But the end came too soon when he was killed by a big country dog in East Hampton.

After that, I couldn't imagine having another dog. I just couldn't. But my husband, Phil, was ready. He kept urging me—pleading, really—and I finally relented. We chose a Golden Retriever because we had a lot of geese on our property and we were told that Goldens would chase them away because they're Retrievers. But none of them ever did. They were completely disinterested.

We ended up with three Goldens: Huey, Louie, and Dewey. It took me awhile to warm up to Huey, who was my first since having my heart broken so badly when my Yorkie died. But Louie softened me up pretty good; and by the time Dewey came into the picture, I was a committed dog lover all over again.

These were great, great dogs. Watching the three of them run around together, jumping up in the air, and throwing things to each other was really wonderful. It was like a ballet. Goldens are such big dogs, yet so graceful—and so human. They were very communicative, too. If they didn't feel well, or if they wanted to play, needed a hug, or were just plain tired, they let you know.

I'll never forget how comforting they were to me when my father died. All three would huddle around me whenever they saw me crying. They'd put their heads against my legs and stare up at me, as if to say, "We're here and we love you." They were so empathetic.

Hughie was the oldest. He was more Phil's dog—whenever Phil got up from a chair, Hughie got up. Wherever Phil walked, Hughie walked. He was Phil's shadow and guardian.

Louie was born from Hughie's mother and uncle. When he arrived two years later, he became my dog. He was just eight months old when I took him on the road with me for a national tour of *Six Degrees of Separation*. Everyone backstage adored Louie and he became the company dog. During the show, he'd stay very quiet. Goldens are so smart. A couple of hours later, when he heard the applause, he knew the show was over and he would come out from under my dressing table and stand by the door, waiting for me to come in. A real stage door Johnnie.

Years later when Louie was older—Huey was already gone then from cancer—we found a tumor in his esophagus. The surgeon wasn't sure he would be able to remove the tumor but we felt we had to give Louie the chance. When we took him to the hospital for the surgery, he looked at me as if to say, "Why are you doing this to me?" I felt so bad, like I was punishing a four-year-old child who didn't quite understand what was going on. We waited for the doctor to come out and tell us the results of the operation. I cried when he said he was able to cut away the tumor. After all, it was an operation for someone I loved, just like any member of my family.

Louie recovered and had a couple more great years but the cancer returned and he grew weaker fast. We couldn't do anything more for him. It was like caring for a very old person who was unable to care for himself. I would hand-feed him because he had so little energy left. He could barely make it outside once a day to do his business.

By that time, Louie wasn't able to climb the stairs anymore when Phil and I would go up for the night. All three of the dogs used to sleep by our bed. With Huey gone, and Louie no longer able to manage the stairs, Dewey wouldn't go either. It was so touching to see that he wouldn't leave his older brother alone at night.

I called the vet, worrying if I should put Louie down. Just because I loved him so much didn't mean I should make him live if he didn't want to. But the vet said that Louie would tell me when. That was such comforting and wise advice.

One morning when I came downstairs, Dewey jumped up as usual to go outside but Louie didn't move. He just looked at me and wouldn't get up. I laid down on the floor next to him for a while. I brought him some porridge I had made and tried to feed him, but he wouldn't take it.

"Louie, are you telling me it's now?" I said to him softly. "Is this it?"

Dewey started running around in circles like he knew what was happening. Phil and I put Louie in a blanket and carried him to the vet, who took one look and said the dog was done. It was time to put him down.

"Just a minute," I said.

I put my head next to Louie's and told him how much we loved him, how he had been such a wonderful part of our family and that we would never forget him. His eyes were closed but he nuzzled his nose next to my face, as I cried and cried. I looked at the vet and nodded. He gave Louie the injection.

It happened so fast. It was the fastest thing I'd ever seen in my life. For Louie's sake, I was glad it was that fast but it was scary to see how quickly you could make a living thing die.

I stayed there a long time with Louie. I didn't want to abandon him. I felt he deserved that. The fur on his face was still wet from my crying on him. You wouldn't leave someone dead in a hospital bed and just walk out. You need time to be there with them for a bit before you are finally able to walk away.

So we put my pal down. Louie had died like an older person whose body simply slows down and can't go on. People and animals try to hold on for as long as they can—they do it for us. And then they can't do it any longer.

Back home, Dewey wouldn't eat for days.

When we had all three dogs, they used to eat from a triangle of three bowls. After Huey died, we put food out for Louie and Dewey, but as they approached their bowls, they suddenly stopped, turned away from them and looked at the space where Huey's bowl used to be. Then they just walked away without eating anything. The vet explained that they were mourning. They'd been together all their lives, and now that the alpha dog was gone they were working it out. They missed a few days of meals. They just wouldn't eat.

Dewey did the same thing when Louie died. He wouldn't eat or leave our side. He became kind of crazy, too, behaving as he'd never done before. Sooner than later, he became sick and was gone, too.

In a span of fourteen years—Hughie, Louie, and Dewey each lived that long—they went from little puppies to old dogs—and so quickly. The arc of life for dogs happens so fast.

It's very emotional when you lose your dog. And so it should be. They're part of your family. Like anyone you've loved—a person or an animal—your heart doesn't know the difference. When the heart loves, it loves. It opens up wide and loves them; and when they leave you, it cracks and breaks.

But the memories are great and full of fun. Our dogs really gave us lots of love, and they received love. We gave them a good life and a good end of life. That was so important to us.

I have many friends who have lost dogs and say that they will never have one again—that they can't go through the heartbreak another time. I understand that feeling. I felt that way at first, too. But you know, it's been about four years since we lost the last one and we're just beginning to talk about getting two more Goldens some time very soon. The heart does heal and makes room for love again.

Marlo Thomas

Why Me?

My bed is gone, my one and only.
My water bowl is gone, the only one I recognize.
My favorite toy is gone, the one I love.
And the human family I have been with for so many years—gone.

Is this shelter cage any place to abandon an old friend?
There isn't a familiar friend here or anywhere else in my life.

I am a homeless senior dog.
I know I am old.
I am more tired than I used to be and I sleep a little bit more.
I don't see as well or hear so good.
But I'm not dead!

I was used to having the run of the house, my head petted, my ears scratched, and belly rubbed.
I knew just when to bark to get the treat I was entitled to or how to stand anxiously by the door,
As if to say, "I'm trying to be patient but hurry up with the leash; I really gotta pee."

Suddenly it is all gone. What did I do wrong?
I'm living in a cage at a shelter.
Potential adopters pass right by me, pausing to let out a sympathetic sigh,
Before moving on to see the younger dogs.

Most of us will not be adopted.
We will live out our remaining years, months or days alone in a cage.
But some people care and run great programs for senior dogs.
Maybe you will find them—and me, too.

Anonymous
Inspired by the White Muzzle Fund

A Reason to Live

My name is Bill Berloni. I am the top theatrical animal trainer on Broadway, having rescued and trained nearly every animal that has played on The Great White Way since 1977, beginning with the original Sandy in the smash hit *Annie*. The original Sandy went on to become the longest running performing animal in Broadway history. In my career, I have rescued hundreds of dogs who went on to play roles in shows like *Annie, The Wizard of Oz, Oliver, Chitty Chitty Bang Bang, Legally Blonde, Gypsy,* and many others. Since beginning this wonderful run in 1977, I have never had less than ten dogs living with me, and over the last twenty years I have continually shared my family home with no less than twenty dogs. Just like their human costars, some animals' careers can last for years while some are done after opening night. But what happens to these canine actors who were once abandoned? The answer is simple; they live with us.

I am an only child. My parents were first generation Italian and German immigrants who taught me to work hard and respect all life. Growing up on a farm in Connecticut, my early companions were my dogs and cats. They made me realize animals were not lesser creatures but sentient beings that had as much right to be happy as we do.

When my career led me to animal training for the entertainment field, my methods of positive reenforcement and humane treatment of animals created a whole new opportunity on Broadway. Taking abandoned animals, giving their life purpose and a job that is fun restores their souls. Not only are they happy and willing to work—they are grateful.

When anyone, human or animals, gives me their all, I am humbled. I have seen dogs want to continue to work in shows even when it hurts to walk. Why? Because if you love what you do, it gives you reason to live. Every time I retire a dog, I know it's going to break their heart. They have lived long lives, happily going to the show each night, soaking up the love the casts give them, and in the end, happy they have pleased me. But when age or ailments make it hard for them to perform, we stop. That's tough. The look they give me when they see our suitcases out and a younger dog going on is heartbreaking. Humans may say they look forward to a retired life with no responsibilities, but animals that are productive and having fun show me what true spirit can really be.

As a trainer, here is when the fun part begins. How do I keep a retired dog feeling like they have a purpose? Simple. Give them a new job. For example, instead of doing a challenging show like *Annie,* we put them in a production of *Of Mice and Men.* In that show, there is an old dog that limps onstage, grabs the audience's sympathy and then gets taken out back and shot. Talk about a walk-on! Or instead of making people smile and laugh on Broadway we go to nursing homes and schools and do pet therapy. One show and they may sleep a week. Sometimes, I create a new sub pack of dogs that the older dog can bully while whipping smaller, young ones into shape. Or instead of chasing wicked witches, they help me corral the chickens. And finally, when they become too tired for their new jobs, they move up to the place of honor in our home—a bed right next to mine where they have all of our one-on-one attention.

At the end of another day of rescuing, training, and rehabbing new dogs, it is always a comfort to sit next to my older dogs that look up to me with their faces full of wisdom, ready to teach me once again how to be a better person. It's as if they are saying, "I have been there, done that. I hoped you learned something from me that you will use on all the newcomers."

The truth is I have learned something from each and every one of them. That makes me the luckiest guy around, to have been able to share their lives, and for that I am truly grateful.

Bill Berloni

Chief

As an adult I never had a dog. I moved to New York City to be a playwright, and the notion of having a dog in the city just seemed too hard for me.

In the 1990s, my partner, John, and I moved to Bucks County, Pennsylvania, to a farmhouse on a small hill. John wanted us to get a dog right away, but we both were commuting into New York City so much that I initially resisted.

However, we had eight acres; and we even had a fenced meadow where the previous owners had kept sheep. So actually this was a great place for a dog. And if not now, when? And even though we had to go to the city often in the day, still other people got dog walkers and worked things out. So I agreed with John, finally, that it was now time to get a dog.

We looked at several shelters. The third one was a non-kill shelter in Milford, New Jersey, just across the river from us in PA. These dogs were lively, and the people working there gave you treats to give the dogs, and encouraged you to walk any dog you felt drawn to.

There were several dogs we walked, friendly mutts. We liked them.

And there was also this Dalmatian. He wasn't in the big cages like the other dogs. He was in this empty, carpeted office. One of the women showing us around explained that this dog was so well house trained that he couldn't go to the bathroom in the little outside part of the cage as the other dogs did. It just didn't feel right to him. So they kept him in this solo office by himself, and they just committed to walking him a few times a day so he could do his business. He had been there about three weeks. He was fully grown, maybe two or three.

We met the dog in this office, and thought he was interesting. He was very calm, not as outgoing as the couple of mutts we had been walking.

So we checked a few more outgoing dogs, but the main person at the shelter said to us, "you should take another look at the Dalmatian, he's a special dog."

John and I took turns giving him a second visit. We went in and sat on the floor with him. He made very good eye contact. He let you hug him. We definitely liked him, though he seemed a tad standoffish.

The shelter was closing in about an hour. John thought we should take this dog. I was leaning toward it, too, but wanted to wait a day or so. Plus we were supposed to visit a friend in Connecticut the next day, and see a Yellow Lab there that needed a home.

As we were about to leave, a rather dolled-up young woman spoke to the shelter worker we had been talking to, and said that she was still interested in the Dalmatian. And mentioned some story about how her previous dog kept running away. We wondered if we would've run away from her, too. And she lived in a city somewhere.

Still, I wasn't ready to make a decision. We left and went to a nearby restaurant. John said he was worried that that woman was going to come back and take the Dalmatian. He thought we should take the dog today. I looked at my watch. The shelter would close in twenty minutes. We paid the check quickly, and went back.

The woman at the shelter said, "Oh, I knew you would come back." And we did the paperwork and took the dog home. John drove, and I sat in the backseat with the dog, putting my arm around him.

We brought him into the house. He was interested but a little disoriented. John always wanted the dog to sleep in the bed with us, but this dog seemed not to want to leave the first floor. Plus our stairs are very eccentric—they're narrow, and they turn midway; so looking up from a dog's perspective, it seemed daunting and confusing that the stairs turned left and then went … where?

We fed the dog and since he just didn't want to go the second floor, we set up a bed for him in the living room. He seemed to feel safer there; and he looked a little like he did in that office. A bit stoic, a bit royal, a bit "I'll just wait and see what happens."

As the evening went on, we encouraged him again to try coming up the stairs, but he just didn't want to. So we left him to stay in his living room quarters, on the blanket on the floor. He seemed content there.

We went to bed and watched TV and went to sleep.

In the morning, we suddenly heard steps on the stairs, and the dog arrived in the room and effortlessly jumped on the bed. After all his hesitations about the stairs, we were amazed at the suddenness of his arrival, and impressed by his dexterity both on the stairs and jumping on the bed.

We called him Chief, named for a Black Lab in Connecticut who used to visit us when we rented there.

A couple of weeks later, John had to go to Ohio to visit his mother and siblings for about six days. It was summer, and I didn't have to go into the city at all. And for the next week, I was with Chief all the time. And he and I bonded very closely.

I remember the second day he was sitting on the bed, and I like to sing, and had this impulse to sing to him a song from the musical *On a Clear Day You Can*

See Forever. The song is called "Hurry, It's Lovely Up Here," and it is an upbeat and welcoming song the main character sings to flowers, encouraging them to grow. I sang the song very quietly, but meaning the lyrics and making eye contact with Chief. He seemed interested and sort of surprised to be sung to. I hugged him after his welcoming song.

For the next many years, how John and I loved that dog. John and I both sing, and John also plays the piano. And one day we were in the kitchen and for reasons I can't recall were singing in a high falsetto to the dog. It was either "I Could Have Danced All Night" or "Danny Boy," but when we got to the higher parts of the song, Chief began to howl in pleasure—though to our surprise, he seemed to be on the same pitch as we. He was hitting the note correctly. This amazed us, and we did it a few more times. Chief seemed to love this, and wagged his tail like crazy when we would all sing together. Of course, it was reminiscent of dogs howling, but still his hitting the correct high note was remarkable.

We didn't do this daily, but when we were feeling playful. Chief was good at learning words, and when we would say "do you want to sing?" he would immediately wag his tail like crazy, and we would start a song and he'd sort of murmur along with us until the high note, at which point he would let loose with his big high note as well. We always chose songs that had a crescendo to them.

Chief didn't like it when we left him alone for the day (though we found wonderful dog walkers to visit with him) but he was very stoic. He would go to my office and sit on the couch, looking sad but resigned.

When we came home, he was such an example to us humans—none of that "Where were you? I expected you hours ago" that we humans say to each other. Chief was always just thrilled to see us. "Hooray, hooray" was the gestalt of his greeting when we came back.

Chief was very healthy for several years. But he started to have sporadic stomach issues—initially we thought it was just eating something bad in the field.

But then one morning—the day before I was supposed to take the dog to Long Island with me for a two-week teaching job I had—Chief became very, very ill. He threw up outside in the grass; and didn't want to come back in. He had to go the dog hospital, and I had to call up and cancel my teaching job, because it was clear that Chief would not be well enough to bring with me any time soon. Luckily the people at the college were dog lovers and very understanding.

Starting here, he had several illnesses in a row—liver, pancreas, and kidney problems. The pancreas was the most serious of the illnesses, but amazingly our vet Ellen found medicines and diet solutions that kept these illnesses at bay, and he was well and happy for most of this period. We feel that Ellen gave us two or three extra years, and we're grateful.

Then, in his tenth year with us, he got a second pancreas ailment called insulinoma. His pancreas was pumping insulin into the blood stream with no rhyme or reason, decimating the sugar in his blood that he needed to function. There was no cure, but the illness could be held at bay (for a while) by giving Chief sugary foods and complex carbohydrates, which release sugar slowly over time.

For a while this worked. Chief had this extremely sticky maple syrup–glop I poured on his food. It gave him a shock of sugar to keep functioning. And he liked it for about a month, but then definitively refused to eat it anymore.

We moved on to honey. He would get a "fading away" look, and I would put some honey on his gums. It would start to make him feel better, and then he'd be willing to lap up a lot of honey from a small bowl I held to his mouth. He could feel himself reviving.

This honey-carb period lasted about two months. Finding what foods he was willing to eat became very stressful. And breakfast and dinner took about an hour each.

Then he started to fade away. And to resist the honey, too. He sat in this one place in the living room. It felt like he was starting to leave.

We brought him to the vet to put him to sleep. I had it in my head that it would be almost soothing when he closed his eyes. But his eyes stayed open. And then when the shot took effect, I could see the life leave his eyes. It was horrible. I guess not horrible, it was heartbreaking. John and I were able to leave the vet's office and go outside, and then sobbed. They brought the dog's body wrapped in a sheet to the car. We had prepared to bury him under a tree near a pond on our property. We got home and put him in the ground.

I hesitate to tell the following because it sounds made up. But the day after we buried Chief, John had to go to some appointment for a few hours. I was alone, and still feeling so sad about Chief. And I went out to where we buried him, and I spoke to him and said I missed him and hoped he was happy. And then I said, not knowing I was going to, "If you can send a sign of any kind I would like that." But I didn't really expect one.

So I went back into that living room where Chief spent his first night. And I had the television on in the background. I was at my computer, and I didn't like the noise from the TV so I switched it to Turner Classic Movies, which I often put on since I love old movies. The channel was showing the film *How the West Was Won*. And suddenly the dialogue I heard was George Peppard saying to Henry Fonda, "Thanks for fixing things with the Chief." And I said out loud, "What???"

Because I have DVR, I was able to rewind and hear that sentence again, so I knew I hadn't made it up. And it was about five minutes after I asked Chief—or the universe—for a sign.

Obviously they're talking about an Indian Chief; and one can say there are coincidences. But I don't know—I have felt at different times in my life that I have gotten messages from the universe, not often, but sometimes. And this sentence occurring the moment I changed the channel of a three-hour-long movie seemed kind of remarkable.

Time has gone by. But how John and I loved that dog. . . .

Christopher Durang

Still My Pup

He was one of the most beautiful animals we had ever seen—muscular, lean, and perfectly proportioned, one of those good-looking guys mothers fuss about when they earnestly present them as loyal, loving, and affable. Even now, his butterscotch coat hangs like a designer suit on an athletic frame. Brad Pitt, said the dog walker. I thought more like Gary Cooper or George Clooney.

My daughter, Lucy, decided he was the complete package when she was five years old and resolved to marry him. You can't marry between species, I said. I could see from her stare that I had missed the point. We looked at wedding dresses. We discussed the pros and cons. It's a little weird to have your husband on a leash, she said.

On the designated night, we gathered in the living room. Waffle sat patiently next to Lucy on the living room floor while her eight-year-old brother, Benny, apparently having watched enough weddings on TV, officiated. Lucy gave Waffle a ring that she attached to his collar and promised her undying love. They had a classic wedding smooch and then Lucy dressed Waffle in a black velvet shirt and he sat at the table with us for ice cream.

That was eight years ago. Waffle is gray on the muzzle now, with frosty fur circling his kind, brown eyes. His gait is slower. He sleeps a lot. But the love he and my daughter share is still going strong.

I asked Lucy how she feels being married to an older man. She said, "It's a little sad when he has trouble getting up onto the bed—but he's still my pup."

Lise Zumwalt

I Found Dogs at Forty-six

I never had a dog growing up. I always had cats. I picked out my first cat when I was four. My friend's cousin had given me a piece of raspberry gum and it fell out of my mouth into a box of kittens and landed on the head of one. So I took her home. Mimi.

Forty-four years later, I got two dogs, Asti and Miko. (There was no gum involved.) Why two? Maybe I was making up for lost time.

This is how it happened: My stepsons had been bargaining with us for two years to get a dog.

"No way," I said, "because I'm going to be the one walking it."

But one day, out of the blue I said, "Let's get two dogs! One for each stepson and they'll keep each other company when we're not home."

It was the craziest and smartest thing I've ever done.

That was three-and-a-half years ago. Because they were rescued we can only guess how old they are and we think they're seven and ten.

Miko, my boy, whose name might actually be Mike (but there was a typo), probably didn't have a very happy puppyhood, so he acts like a seven-year-old (in dog years) and I think he'll always be like that.

Asti, my girl, is older and bigger—the alpha. She was an old soul when we got her. She's deep. I can tell she has seen a lot in her life. She reminds me of people I have known. And of Mimi. I also think she's trying to poison me with her gases.

I have found it impossible to teach my old dogs new tricks, old tricks, any tricks. But I can't imagine my life without Asti and Miko, even though I'm the one walking them. There is no love like loving your dog.

Wendy Liebman

Another Sort of Love Story

Right in the middle of a long New Year's weekend full of bright weather on lovely snow and a numbing succession of televised quarterbacks, our dog died. Or to put it absolutley straight, after a family agreement rare in its unannimity, we had his life stopped by a veterinarian who agreed it was the right thing to do for such a painfully and fatally ill old animal. His name was John Henry, but I'm not sure why we'd called him that.

I don't think I have ever been more sharply aware of the fine line between here and gone than I was near the end when I held him close on the vet's table. The kind doctor, her eyes floating in tears because she knew him and us, pumped something bluish into his leg, and with the calm, open-eyed patience that characterized so much of his style, he waited that briefest moment until it struck his center and killed him. A couple of polite gasps and it was over.

Slightly undone by my sentiment and for some wild reason remembering not *Lassie* but *Love Story* and the astounding communicative success of Erich Segal, I will risk a version of his opening question: what can you say about an eleven-and-a-half-year-old dog that died? That he was at least as beautiful as Ali MacGraw. And dumber. And a messier eater. That he ran shining and marvelously fast through fields and rolled snorting in snow and floated a burnt-auburn blur over stone walls. That he didn't much mind Mozart and Bach but that violin solos and harmonicas made him howl. That he could destroy six glasses with one sweep of his tail. That, when I would ask him how he ranked me among the people he liked, he would thump his tail against the floor and grin, occassionally punctuating that with a noise that became a smell. But he was half Irish Setter and half Golden Retriever, and his manners were predictably imperfect.

There was a totally nonhuman quality in his loving. Virtually everyone was a suitable target for his affection, and unlike your one-man brute who will slobber over his master's hand and then dismember the neighbor's child, he menaced nothing, including the rabbits he chased and never got and the skunks who always got him.

Not that he was indiscriminating. He was not a tramp, and he did not follow strangers. He was a wide-ranging country dog, but his daily investigations brought him home again at night. He liked to sleep on rugs, usually where it was convenient to stumble over him. He liked to ride in cars. Best, he liked to be invited along on walks, and he worked like a roving scout around the walker—in front, behind, alongside, often at a dead run a good distance away—and when he rested in winter during one of these wonderful dashes in all directions, he would break ice in a stream to cool his belly and his tongue.

Although he was forced to live with a succession of cats, I don't think he liked them at all. Yet in most moods but joy he was a model of understatement. The weary and wary tolerance he displayed at the cats' rude spitting or at their hit-and-run assaults from ambush beneath a chair was the closest he came to expressing real distaste.

Obviously our knowledge is limited about his relationship with other dogs. He probably had wet down bark or bush with every dog within a radius of three miles, but he didn't seem to care much for groups, preferring to run alone or with just one other at a time. He was alert and forward but not aggressive, and though his hair bristled splendidly and he growled well when challenged, he had a disctinct aptitude for avoiding fights and could walk away from one with a casualness that implied it wouldn't be worth his trouble. In his late years he was treated roughly by a much younger and stronger dog down the road, but he accepted this indignity in a way that wasn't cowardly, as if it were somehow in the normal order of things that the puppy he had earlier taught to play was now bouncing him around quite badly. Even when he was very feeble and old, he always trotted out to defend his home station.

I hope he had a full and happy sex life, but I know only one affair; it was arranged and he fathered a litter from it. His partner in this matter was a bitch from the household of good friends. She, too, was sweet and easygoing and she looked more or less as if she came from a similarly mixed background. We tell a story about this match and I am no longer sure whether it is entirely true. The story goes that, oblivious of approaching delight, he was taken by car to the vet's for one suprervised meeting. The vet said afterward that he felt certain everything had gone well, but perhaps for insurance the two should be brought together again the next day. So next day our dog was put in the car and driven to his appointment, which was once more declared a success. The affair was pronounced consummated—and closed. The dog came home. The following morning he was found ready in the car, presumably awaiting another trip and another meeting.

Unlike Segal's doomed creature, this one wasn't perfect. Now and then his taste in food would turn to garbage and he upset many cans in search for the ripest morsels. He dug holes in lawns and he liked to sprawl on young plants. He was a discoverer of mud. When he found something—often invisible and even nonexistent—to bark at, he barked hard and he utterly ignored commands to stop it and come the hell home. I am proud of one area of his ignorance. He knew no tricks at all, unless you count a sort of half-baked pawshake he employed as a last effort in his perpetual and undiscouraged search for affection.

In his last days he had great difficulty getting up, he tottered weakly on three legs and he was dreadfully thin. The pain, even muffled with pills, was leaving him stupid with exhaustion, and it became clear past all reluctance that he needed a push out of life. Briefly, I had the conventional and outlandish thought of doing it myself, and so did one of my sons, who likely loved the dog most. Then, with her potion that hit with such shocking and merciful speed, the doctor ended our nonsense.

That night I dreamed that my son kept calling him. The boy had a way of calling that dog. I woke. Life gets to be a series of dogs, I thought, and I ticked off those I could remember. Ghosts in the house suddenly. Old dogs. When I slept and woke again, it was cold half-light and I was almost sure I heard the dog's toenails against the hall floor and his single, discreet bark to go outside. I won't live with a lot more dogs, and I won't live with another dog like him.

Loudon Wainwright

In Praise of Senior Dogs

The Benefits of Adopting a More Mature Companion

When I first saw Rooney at the Martinez, California, animal shelter, she was dazed, matted, and unsteady—obviously on her last legs. Her breath could've fueled my car. As a dog rescuer, I kicked myself for agreeing to see her. What possible prospects could I offer this bedraggled old Border Collie, beyond a marginally better demise?

Within two months (and minus several bad teeth), she was adopted—and seven years later, just after her passing, I look back on her as one of my all-time favorite success stories.

Named for her resemblance to *60 Minutes* commentator Andy, she was a grand old gal, full of nobility, life, and love. She was gentle with adults and grandkids, she respected cats, and she kept younger dogs in line, even with that half-empty maw. Rooney was quick to settle into a regular routine, and when you patted her she just oozed gratitude and affection. In short, she was the perfect companion for Margie, the empty nester who adopted her. The world would have been poorer if those two hadn't matched up and devoted themselves to each other.

If you're approaching your AARP years (or even if you're far from it), you've probably read about the many health benefits of pet ownership. Study after study has shown that blood pressure goes down, cholesterol levels improve, and even heart attack risk declines. Companion animals may be the antiaging medicine that you really should "ask your doctor about." Having a pet also encourages you to get out and exercise, even if it's just a gentle daily walk. And statistics don't count the warmth, companionship, and pure love that a mature canine can bring into a household.

Adult dogs are settled into their personalities, so you know what you're getting more than you would with a puppy or yearling. They are usually house-trained, and may already know basic commands like "sit" and "stay." Contrary to the old adage, you *can* teach these dogs new tricks. With adolescence out of their systems, they tend to focus pretty well on teaching moments. Their desire to please their people is very well ingrained.

And I can't prove it, but I've heard it said too many times to discount, the notion that adult adoptees are just plain grateful. They've seen the world's harsher side and seem particularly appreciative of the new lease on life they've been given.

I recall an older gentleman who was looking over some impossibly cute foster puppies. Asked where he planned to be in ten years, he replied, smiling, "Dirt nap!" With many breeds' life expectancies in the twelve to eighteen year range (smaller being typically longer lived), six- or seven-year-old dogs—and even teenagers like Rooney, still have plenty of good "treadlife" on them. My senior friend decided on an eight-year-old Lab mix, and they've never looked back. (And I know Margie wouldn't trade her years with Rooney for anything. She's since taken in Gloria, another senior grand dame.)

A shelter in Reno recently received a letter from a woman who had adopted a senior dog there some time ago and then returned for another. She wrote: "Frankie's time with me was very good. He was loving, gentle, and a good friend. I want to tell you that I think I needed Frankie more than he needed me, but he loved me and I was grateful for that wonderful creature every day that I had him. My new girl, Willow, is lying at my feet chewing on a rawhide. I hope this makes sense—I heard her snore last night while I was watching television. I can hear her breathe and I am not so alone."

Sitting here with that story fresh in my mind, where it shares space with fond memories of Rooney, I am gratified to know that these adoptions can hold such meaning and enrich the lives of all concerned. If you have a hankering for "one more good dog," please consider adopting an older best friend—it's one of the biggest win-win opportunities that senior life affords.

It is possible that animals are our greatest gifts in this life.

Tom Cushing

A Senior Dog? My Little Puppy?
You Must Be Kidding!

How did this happen? Who is that, looking back at me in the mirror, with that smug, confused look on his face? Excuse me while I pretend I don't recognize myself, aging right in front of my eyes. Of course I know I am, and the gray hair and "fine lines" belong to me, but accepting it is a whole other matter.

I don't think I'm alone with this. Most people dance their way through middle age on the tipping point between illusion and reality. And it's the same with our dearly beloved dogs. As they age, we don't want to admit it to ourselves.

When I jokingly asked a friend who had recently joined the AARP if there is an equivalent organization for her senior dogs, she became indignant.

"My dogs are not seniors!" she cried. "They don't even act old. They scamper and leap and play around just like always."

According to the American Animal Hospital Association, dogs generally lived seven or eight years back in the 1970s. Now, those life spans have reached ten to fifteen years. Certain breeds, mixed breeds, and smaller dogs tend to live even longer.

But it's important to know—and accept—when your particular dog might qualify as a senior. Learning more will help you understand the changes in behavior your dog may be showing or to anticipate a change in their health. Knowledge becomes a matter of prevention and preparing wisely for the inevitable.

A Tufts University study reveals the following guidelines for defining a senior dog: "The point at which a dog qualifies as 'aged' varies. Veterinarians generally consider small dogs to be senior citizens at about 12 years of age, while large dogs reach the senior stage at 6 to 8 years of age. This roughly corresponds to the 55-plus category in people."

But just because you witness your dog acting differently, for example taking longer to get up from a sitting position or laboring up the stairs, doesn't mean he is a senior yet. These may simply be symptoms of an illness requiring treatment and could have nothing to do with aging.

Sound familiar?

Veterinarians concur that diseases affect older dogs in ways that rarely trouble younger ones. The potential for arthritis, diabetes, Cushing's disease, cancer, and kidney, heart, and liver diseases increases as a dog ages, just as they do in humans. This can be revealed in blood tests, but owners can also help by providing a healthy diet, regular exercise, clean teeth, and a regimen of consistent check-ups.

Other factors that influence your older dog's aging process and may contribute to eventual age-related problems are genetics, which vary by breed, nutrition, and the environment.

But like it or not, just like each of us, our dogs are getting older and it behooves us to pay attention and take care of them as best as we can. If you're not sure how, there are many organizations dedicated to providing the information you'll need to preserve the health of your senior dog.

And don't forget—an aging dog needs a healthy owner.

David Tabatsky

An Old Dog's Lament

I'm sorry I'm not cute anymore.
I'm so sorry I got all big and old and you got tired of me.
I'm sorry you don't have time to play with me
and think I'm more trouble than I'm worth.
It must be my fault that things turned out this way.
Please forgive me.
Please tell me how to be cute again.
Please don't throw me away.

Anonymous

Larger than Life

Garry and I once took a winter walk with a Golden Labrador puppy he was training. It was her first time in the snow and she rolled around excitedly in the fresh blanket of white until her fur was completely wet. She raced around, licking icicles dangling from storefronts. When I remember that puppy's unbridled exuberance, I think of Garry. Fun and charming, he could also be quite irreverent. He loved intellectual conversation and a good debate. A fervent atheist, Garry and I often argued about spirituality and the very existence of the soul.

Garry admired great beauty and intellect, whether it was in a human being or a dog. While he enjoyed training smart dogs that were quick to learn, he loved a good challenge, fearlessly working with dogs that had serious issues. Older dogs especially drew out a very gentle and vulnerable side of Garry. Ostensibly, he was the one training the dogs, but I often thought he was learning a lot from them as well, from perseverance and patience to unconditional love and compassion, for them and for himself.

As Garry struggled with his own aging process, he increasingly identified with the plight of older dogs. They moved him. They were noble and wise, not frail and diminished with age. Garry found beauty in imperfection and strength in vulnerability and he tried to capture those profound and elusive qualities in his photos.

Garry recognized something special in each of these senior dogs. He saw the glimmer in their eyes and the beauty in their souls. And with his perfect touch, he made them larger than life.

Branka Ruzak

Beau

People talk nonsense to dogs all the time, the same as they talk to babies. I whispered in his ear over and over again, the way I had when he was a puppy squatting on the grass. "Yes, yes, you are the man," I murmured, "you are the best dog, yes, everything's going to be all right, you are the man." Dr. Brown looked at me and I nodded and she pushed the plunger on the syringe. Beau took two deep growly breaths and then he fell onto me. We had put him down. I don't like euphemisms for death, hate the term "passed away" for someone who has died, but the expression we use for dogs is the right one. We put him down.

I've never really believed what people say, that death smooths the lines of life away, that the tension and the worry disappear. Yet somehow after the vet had packed up and the children had gone, Beau did look more like his old self, before his legs and eyesight and hearing began to go. He looked more like the kind of dog who would try to drive a horse from his stretch of the road, or swim in circles, his tail a feathered rudder, in pursuit of geese. He looked like one of those handsome Labs on the cover of a dog book. He looked like what he was: a really good dog.

The life of a good dog is like the life of a good person, only shorter and more compressed. In the fifteen years since Beau had joined our family, nine pounds of belly fat and needle teeth, he had grown ancient by the standards of his breed. And I had grown older. My memory stutters. My knees hurt. Without my reading glasses the words on a page look like ants at a picnic. But my blood pressure is low, my bone scan is good, and my mammograms are so far uneventful. I love my kids, and they love me, and we all love their father, who is still my husband. Starting out, I thought that life was terribly complex, and in some ways it is. But contentment can be pretty simple.

And that's what I learned from watching Beau over his lifetime: to roll with the punches (if not in carrion), to take things as they come, to measure myself not in terms of the past or the future but of the present, to raise my nose in the air from time to time and, at least metaphorically, holler, "I smell bacon!" I'm not what I once was, and neither, by the end, was he. The geese are making a mess of the pond, and the Yellow Lab gets to run every morning with her master. The first couple of times she was walked by herself were particularly sad. Bea misses Beau terribly, I suspect, but I may just be projecting again.

Each morning I used to check to see if the old guy was actually breathing, and each day I tried to take his measure—was he hurting? Was he happy? Was the trade-off between being infirm and being alive worth it? And when the time comes to ask myself some of those same questions, at least I will have had experience calibrating the answer. Sometimes an old dog teaches you new tricks.

Anna Quindlen

Resources for Care and Custody

Would you like to get involved with senior dogs? Are you interested in doing more than reading a book? Perhaps you need help with your own senior-dog issues. Maybe you'd like to become part of a community of volunteers.

The organizations included here are doing great work rescuing, adopting, and caring for senior dogs, as well as partnering them with senior citizens and other folks in need of companionship. These groups—on local, regional, and national levels—offer terrific resources, whether you are searching for help with your own older canine companion or looking to contribute to the work of an organization dedicated to the health and welfare of these valuable and loving animals.

Animal groups that take on the specific responsibility of rescuing senior dogs are few and far between. It is rare to find people willing to open their hearts and homes to senior dogs for adoption or lifetime foster care.

Adopt a Senior Pet of Adopt-A-Pet.com
www.adopt-a-senior-pet.adoptapet.com

The "Adopt a Senior Pet" section of Adopt-A-Pet.com is a nonprofit Senior Pet adoption service sponsored by Purina and Advantage pet foods. Their pet finder search engine allows visitors to enter a location anywhere in the United States with details about the kind of dog he or she is a looking for and it then displays photos of dogs that match that criteria. When visitors click on a dog they like, they receive information about the dog and how to contact the organization offering the animal for adoption.

All Dogs Welcome (ADW)
www.alldogswelcome.com

ADW is dedicated to helping dogs enjoy their humans by assuring that they have all the information they need to keep their animals safe, healthy, and happy.

The Web site includes blogs, information about rescues and shelters, links and information regarding kennel clubs, breeds, and pet locating services nationwide.

A dog with a medical problem or an aging dog can still be a lovable and loving member of a household. That owners can even consider surrendering their dogs due to age, injury, or health issues is beyond comprehension. But it happens. And all too often these dogs are further insulted by being considered unadoptable by the shelters to which they've been surrendered. They are usually scheduled for almost immediate euthanasia.

ADW will link you to a nationwide list of organizations that specialize in the rescue, care, and placement of senior pets.

All Pets Wellness Foundation

www.allpetswellnessfoundation.org

Based in Illinois, All Pets Wellness Foundation was founded by a group of dedicated advocates to provide funds to care for sick and injured pets for owners who cannot afford it. This is a particular need for owners of senior dogs. All Pets insures that people won't have to say good-bye to their pets, either by giving them up or euthanizing them, just because they can't afford treatments. Veterinarians receive grants to assist clients unable to pay for an ailing pet's care.

According to founder Mary Ann Minick, "Another goal of the foundation is to educate pet owners to make sure they know what's available to them. It informs people about pet trusts, care credit, and pet insurance so pet owners won't get to the point where they need additional help from the foundation or any organization."

American Society for the Prevention of Cruelty to Animals

www.aspca.org

Founded in 1866, the ASPCA was the first humane organization in the Western Hemisphere. Our mission, as stated by founder Henry Bergh, is "to provide effective means for the prevention of cruelty to animals throughout the United States." The ASPCA works to rescue animals from abuse, pass humane laws, and share resources with shelters nationwide. There are many ways an animal lover can make a difference. From assisting in the care and placement of shelter animals to educating the public on animal welfare issues to fighting for stronger animal legislation—here are nine ways you can make a difference for animals in your community.

Learn how to report animal cruelty.
Start a neighborhood watch program.
Volunteer at your loal shelter or animal rescue organization.
Become an animal activist.
Help your neighbors help their animals.
Start a pet food bank.
Promote spaying and neutering.
Clean up for wildlife.
Become an ASPCA Ambassador and fund-raise for animals.

Canada's Guide to Dogs
www.facebook.com/CanadasGuideToDogs

A dog-related information Web site that features more than two hundred breeds of dogs, listings of more than twenty-five hundred breeders, rescuers, trainers, and other pet-related services/businesses.

Citizens for Pets in Condos
www.petsincondos.org

Citizens for Pets in Condos, Inc., educates the public in Florida on the health benefits of animal companionship and the value of responsible pet ownership. We believe that association rules in common interest ownership communities should concentrate on irresponsible pet owners, allowing a win-win situation for responsible animal guardians and animals who would otherwise be needlessly euthanized.

Cocker Spaniel Adoption Center
www.cocker.adoption.org

The aim of the Cocker Spaniel Adoption Center in Maryland is to help needy Cocker Spaniels find loving homes. We are frequently called to rescue older dogs. They are so special and dear. To know them is to fall completely in love. If only more people would give them a chance.

Dachshund Adoption Rescue and Education
www.facebook.com/DareToRescue

Some people say, "An older dog up for adoption must have problems, or it wouldn't need rescuing." The reality is that pets enter shelters and rescue societies for every imaginable reason. Often it's not the dog that has the problem, but the human.

Many people get a dog because it seems like the thing to do, not because they truly appreciate the qualities—and needs—of the animal. Others are forced to surrender their pets for personal reasons. There may be a problem with a particular dog, but you are much less likely to find a senior dog that isn't housebroken or a senior dog that snaps; older dogs have usually overcome any bad habits they had when they were young.

Others say, "An older dog will have more medical bills." To some extent, this may be true, in that older dogs need more medical supervision, such as geriatric testing during their annual exams. But there is no health guarantee for a dog of any age. One-year-old dogs can die of cancer. And puppies have larger immediate medical bills because of their need for vaccinations and spay/neuter surgery. And don't forget the bills for chewed shoes and shredded drapes!

Grey Muzzle Organization

www.greymuzzle.org

Based in Raleigh, North Carolina, The Grey Muzzle Organization improves the lives of at-risk senior dogs by providing funding and resources to animal shelters, rescue organizations, sanctuaries, and other nonprofit groups nationwide.

Grey Muzzle is not a shelter; it supports programs across the country in hospice care, senior dog adoption, medical screening, and more. All funds are distributed through grants, provided through fund-raising efforts and the generosity of public donations.

Since 2008, Grey Muzzle has provided over $160,000 in grants for senior dog programs, ranging from $500 to $4,000, to 30 nonprofit organizations in more than seventeen states. Our online store sells gifts and books and designates all profits for at-risk senior dogs. *We believe old dogs contribute positively to our quality of life and have much to teach us about patience, respect, responsibility, loyalty, and unconditional love. We believe every senior dog deserves to live out their golden years, months, weeks or even days in a place of love, security, and peace. We believe in honest and open decision making that allows us to be accountable to our donors and the organizations we support. We envision a world where no old dog dies alone and afraid.*

The Humane Society of the United States

www.humanesociety.org

Backed by 11 million supporters in the United States and around the world, The HSUS is leading the way to a better future for all animals. We advocate for better laws to protect animals; conduct campaigns to reform industries; provide animal rescue and emergency response; investigate cases of animal cruelty; and care for animals through our sanctuaries and wildlife rehabilitation centers, emergency shelters, and clinics. Note: Many local Humane Societies have their own senior dog programs, such as:

The Hinsdale Humane Society

www.hinsdalehumansociety.org

The Berkeley East Bay Humane Society Golden Paws Program

www.berkeleyhumane.org

Escondido Humane Society

www.escondidohumanesociety.org

"Each year, November marks national Adopt-a-Senior Pet Month," says Katie Woolsey, Public Relations Coordinator at the Escondido (CA) Humane Society. "Sadly, older, homeless pets are often overlooked for their younger counterparts, and many people shy away from adopting senior pets because they are afraid of how soon they might lose them. But every animal needs and deserves love—even older ones. Their lives, and yours, will be richer for helping these precious pets live out their golden years in loving homes."

Muttville Senior Dog Rescue
www.muttville.org/resources

Voted "Favorite San Francisco Charity" in *7X7 Magazine*, The Insider's Guide to the Best of San Francisco, Muttville's mission is to change the way the world thinks about and treats older dogs and to create better lives for them through rescue, foster, adoption, and hospice. On a local level in California, Muttville rescues senior dogs and finds them new homes or gives them hospice. On a global level, Muttville provides information about caring for older dogs and support for people who do.

In 2012, Muttville's "Seniors for Seniors" program received a large grant from the Doris Day Animal Foundation. "When we learned about Muttville and its successful rescues of so many senior dogs, we knew we had to help," Miss Day said from her home in Carmel, California.

Nike Animal Rescue Foundation Seniors for Seniors Program
www.narfrescue.org/adopt/seniors-for-seniors-adoption-program

The Nike Animal Rescue Foundation (no connection to the shoe manufacturer) is located in San Jose, California, and is dedicated to the rescue and care of abandoned, feral, and unwanted pets. Our Seniors for Seniors Adoption Program places senior pets with senior citizens. The dog gets a stay-at-home mom or dad to spoil them, and the individual gets an adoring and grateful pet whose expectation is to be the center of the person's universe. Not a bad trade.

North Shore Animal League America Seniors for Seniors Program
www.animalleague.org/adopt-a-pet/pet-adoption-services/seniors-for-seniors/

Headquartered in Port Washington, New York, The North Shore Animal League America (NSALA) is the world's largest no-kill animal rescue and adoption organization. We have created a national network of shelter and rescue partners and are a trusted source for information, education, and resources that increase adoptions and enhance the lives of adopters and their pets.

The Seniors for Seniors Program Adoption Counselors help a senior adopter find the perfect match and offers qualifying seniors with tremendous benefits to help care for their new best friend: no adoption fee, two free groomings annually, and 10 percent off all products at the NSALA Pet Store. It also provides the following health benefits (at the NSALA Medical Center only): no exam or medical co-pay within the first fifteen days after the animal is adopted, free annual vaccinations, free semiannual wellness exam, discounts on preventative procedures, and discounts on diagnostic tests (lab report, screening tests). Interested parties who are unable to adopt or foster animals may support their work by becoming sponsors.

Old Dog Haven

www.olddoghaven.org

Old Dog Haven is a network of private homes helping western Washington's homeless senior dogs. We place senior dogs in foster homes or adopt them out. Volunteers also transport dogs from place to place.

"We need advocates for senior dogs in all sorts of places. It's difficult for shelters and it breaks everyone's hearts. We need to encourage more places for senior dogs to go. We get calls from shelters all over the country, fifty times per week, to take dogs."

Paws for Purple Hearts (PPH)

www.pawsforpurplehearts.org

Founded in 2006 as a program of California's Bergin University for Canine Studies, Paws for Purple Hearts has operated its intensive training programs at four locations throughout the United States: Palo Alto/Menlo Park VA Medical Center (California), Walter Reed National Military Medical Center (Bethesda, Maryland), the National Intrepid Center of Excellence (Bethesda, Maryland), and Fort Belvoir (Virginia).

It is the first program of its kind to offer therapeutic intervention for veterans and active-duty military personnel by teaching those with post-traumatic stress disorder (PTSD) to train service dogs for their comrades with combat-related physical disabilities. PPH is built upon the trusted and time-honored tradition of veterans helping veterans.

PAWS Seniors for Seniors Adoption Program

www.paws.org/seniors-for-seniors.html

With a shelter in Lynnwood, Washington, PAWS' Seniors for Seniors Adoption Program serves greater Seattle. This adoption program promotes senior humans' rediscovery of the joys of having a pet in their lives and places senior cats and dogs (typically over seven years of age) with senior citizens who are sixty years of age or older.

The program helps seniors select a companion who fits into his or her lifestyle and housing situation at a reduced adoption rate.

If an individual becomes unable to take care of his or her new pet due to long-term hospitalization or transfer to a nursing facility, the animal may be returned to PAWS.

Peace of Mind Dog Rescue

www.peaceofminddogrescue.org

Peace of Mind Dog Rescue (POMDR) in Pacific Grove, California, is dedicated to finding new loving homes for dogs whose senior guardians can no longer care for them due to illness, death, or other challenging circumstances, and to finding homes for senior dogs in animal shelters. Their mission is to model lifetime care for dogs and all companion animals to help bring about a positive change in the way society thinks about and treats senior dogs and to create better lives for them through rescue, foster, adoption, and education. Dogs that come into POMDR's care either live out their lives in one of its foster homes or are adopted into a permanent home.

Pedigree Foundation
www.pedigreefoundation.org

Associated with Pedigree® Brand Food for Dogs, The Pedigree Foundation helps dogs who end up in shelters and breed-rescue organizations by providing grants to nonprofit shelters and rescue groups and by encouraging dog adoption. Donations to the Foundation go directly to select shelters and breed rescues nationwide.

In 2011, the Pedigree® brand committed to match the total contributions the Foundation received up to $500,000.

In 2010, The Pedigree Foundation made over eleven hundred operation grants in an average amount of $650.00 and ten innovation grants in an average amount of $22,600.

The Foundation and Brand has raised more than $5 million to date.

Pets for the Elderly Foundation
www.petsfortheelderly.org

Active in over fifty-two shelters in twenty-nine states, The Pets for the Elderly Foundation believes that the most serious disease for older persons is not cancer or heart disease. It's loneliness. Pets offer affection, unconditional love, fight loneliness, and can help ease the loss of a loved one. The Pets for the Elderly Foundation helps pay the fees to participating animal shelters throughout the United States for senior citizens (age sixty and over) who adopt a companion dog or cat from a participating shelter—including pre-adoption veterinary exams and spay/neuter, if part of the adoption fee. Assisting older individuals this way not only saves the life of an animal, it can also make a dramatic difference in the life of an elderly person. A complete list of participating shelters is available at our Web site.

The Sanctuary for Senior Dogs
www.sanctuaryforseniordogs.org

Located in Cleveland, Ohio, The Sanctuary works to rescue abandoned senior dogs and provide them lifelong quality care. We host Adoption Sunday, when foster dogs and their caregivers gather in their Adoption & Education Center so that potential adopters can learn about the dogs from the people who take care of them. Our Companions program brings senior dogs and senior people together. For those unable to foster or adopt a senior dog, The Sanctuary offers the Forever Fosters program, where individuals may sponsor a dog in need who is cared for at the Sanctuary.

Senior Canine Rescue Society (Canada)
www.petfinder.com/shelters/AB01.html

Senior Canine Rescue Society is a nonprofit organization providing a voice for those special members of the pet population who cannot speak for themselves. Since 1997, we have been dedicated to the rescue and rehabilitation of senior and special needs dogs. We are inspired by the zest for life shown by older dogs thrown away in the twilight of their lives, and it is our mission to do what we can to ensure their safe and happy retirement.

We run two e-mail lists for Senior and Special Needs Dogs and have excellent cross posting power—SaSNDR@yahoogroups.com and RescueSeniorDogs@yahoogroups .com. Please join us!

Senior Dogs on Facebook
www.facebook.com/groups/210118748883

For those interested in contacting others informally and discussing issues related to senior dogs, Facebook has an open group that anyone may join.

The Senior Dogs Project
www.srdogs.com

The Senior Dogs Project site is a great starting point if you are looking for a dog to adopt or seeking help in placing a dog through an agency. It presents an inclusive list of animal welfare organizations that help rehome senior dogs, from Bide-a-Wee in New York City to the Homer, Alaska Animal Shelter and everything in between, including local Human Society chapters (many have their own senior dog programs). Agencies are organized by location to enable you to find one nearby. There is also a section devoted to individual breeds. The Project's agency directory also includes photographs and descriptions of specific dogs available for adoption from some of the agencies listed. In addition, the Project provides health care information on senior dogs, which is updated frequently and, although it is limited in scope, it addresses the main conditions, diseases, medicines, and therapies that are relevant to senior dogs.

Silver Paws Program of Atlanta Animal Rescue Friends, Inc.
www.silverpawsprogram.org

The Silver Paws Program connects mature pet lovers with homeless mature pets. Silver Paws foster parents participate in foster orientations and trainings with other fosters, which can serve as an antidote to the isolation many mature adults face.

The program covers the cost of veterinary care, food, and supplies for the foster pets, alleviating the financial concerns that are common.

Since it may take many months or years for an older pet to become adopted, the program allows Silver Paws foster parents to become permanent caretakers for their pets. In these cases, the program will continue to pay for costs associated with the pet, but the dog or cat will no longer be available for adoption. The pet will remain in the care of the foster for the remainder of the pet's life, or until the foster can no longer care for the pet. This provides a caring, permanent home for a mature pet and a loving companion for a mature adult.

Stray Rescue of St. Louis
www.strayrescue.org

Stray Rescue's sole purpose is to rescue stray animals in need of medical attention, restore them to health, and place them in loving adoptive homes. Although we serve only the St. Louis, Missouri, area, a number of our programs may serve as prototypes for other organizations. Our Seniors for Seniors Program enables senior citizens who adopt an older dog to do so without paying the adoption fee, and, if necessary, Stray Rescue will provide food and medical care for the life of the dog. In addition, a person who adopts a senior dog with a chronic health problem may be eligible for complimentary veterinarian support for the ongoing medical condition their dog requires.

Tony La Russa's Animal Rescue Foundation (ARF)
www.arf.net

ARF saves the lives of countless animals each year whose time has run out in public shelters and who are scheduled to be killed. ARF's team of trained volunteers and expert staff make sure every animal receives proper nutrition, medical evaluation and treatment, training, and lots of love as they await their new forever home. ARF's shelter touches the lives of thousands of animals and people each year.

White Muzzle Fund
www.whitemuzzlefund.org

Based in New York City, The White Muzzle Fund is an endowment supporting senior dog rescue programs nationwide that provide loving homes for abandoned older dogs.

Our mission is to provide the means so that abandoned senior dogs will not have

to live out their lives alone in animal shelter cages. We work to create a nationwide network of senior dog rescue programs by providing financial support for existing programs that find loving homes or provide a homelike setting for old dogs. We also initiate and support similar programs where none exist.

The White Muzzle Fund awards grants to nonprofit organizations to specifically support their senior dog programs. These programs are carefully screened and researched to make sure that the senior dogs they help are living in a home or homelike environment with a high level of human interaction. We support senior dog adoptions, lifetime foster care, retirement living, assisted living, and hospice.

Less than 10 percent of general, unrestricted donations go toward White Muzzle Fund expenses, such as operations and fund-raising. The rest goes permanently into the White Muzzle Fund endowment, to generate support for senior dog rescue programs.

Our Honorary Trustee Board includes Kevin Bacon, Kyra Sedgwick, Kim Basinger, Candice Bergen, Anjelica Huston, and Norah Jones.

Wordpress *Senior Dogs Blog*
www.seniordogs.com/wordpress

This blog has articles archived back to October 2009, grouped by medical categories (arthritis, diet, exercise, medications) as well as more general topics. The blog is a "one-stop-shop to find all the best information for your senior dog. There is a vast library of senior dog articles and information on senior dog food, senior dog arthritis, senior dog supplements, senior dog allergies, senior dog medications, senior dog rescue groups, and pet insurance just to name a few."

Contributors

Ellisa Levant Beaver
Ellisa is a graduate of UCSB. She has raised eight dogs through old age and cannot imagine life without a dog in it. Ellisa has two children and currently lives in San Diego, California, with her husband of twenty-three years. Contact at: ellisa@cox.net.

Bill Berloni
For more than thirty years, Bill has provided animals trained to meet the demands of live performances, from Broadway to ballet, as well as film, television, and commercial work. His pioneering humane training techniques have won multiple awards. Bill is the Behavior Consultant for the Humane Society of New York, a no-kill shelter that supports rescued animals in New York City.

Suzanne Clothier
Suzanne has been working with animals since 1977, with experience in obedience, agility, puppy testing, breeding, Search and Rescue, conformation, instructing, kennel management, and canine midwifery. An award-winning author, Suzanne has written for magazines around the world. Her book, *Bones Would Rain from the Sky: Deepening Our Relationships with Dogs* has received wide spread praise from every corner of the dog world, including two inclusions in the *Wall Street Journal*'s list of Top 5 Dog Books.

Tom Cushing
An attorney by trade, Tom Cushing has fed his soul by fostering some 150 dogs over a decade. In 2010, he joined the Nevada Humane Society as associate director, and later helped convert the Alameda, California, animal shelter to a nonprofit operation. Tom lives near San Francisco with his fiancée and four Border Collies.

Doris Day
America's quintessential "girl next door" continues to be revered by her fans, while the media still celebrate her as a legendary Hollywood actress and singer. But Doris's enduring popularity also comes from her devotion to animal welfare. She was one of the founders of Actors and Others for Animals, which remains a leader in the protection of animals in Hollywood. Doris started the Doris Day Pet Foundation in the late 1970s, dedicated to finding homes for the too many animals being destroyed simply because there weren't enough good homes. She formed the Doris Day Animal League to deal directly with elected officials on every level. The DDAL is now partnered with the Humane Society of the United States and continues to be a leading advocacy organization. Doris received the Medal of Freedom, the highest civilian award in the United States, in recognition of her nonprofit work.

Steve Duno

Steve, veteran pet behaviorist, has to date authored eighteen books and scores of magazine and Web articles. He has covered a wide variety of subject matter on both dogs and cats, including basic training, aggression, environmental enrichment, behavior modification, breed profiling, trick training, pet health care, and memoir. Formerly a teacher in New York City and Los Angeles, he currently lives in Seattle with his family and an ever-changing assortment of rescued pets. Steve also writes and publishes short stories, and was a top-ten finalist in the 2003 Glimmertrain Short Story Competition and a finalist in the 2005 Perigee Arts Fiction Contest, in which he garnered an honorable mention award.

Christopher Durang

Christopher is a playwright whose plays have been produced on and off-Broadway, around the country and abroad. They include *Beyond Therapy, Sister Mary Ignatius Explains It All For You, The Marriage of Bette and Boo, Baby with the Bathwater, Laughing Wild,* and *A History of the American Film. Keywords:* satire, dark comedy, parody, funny, absurdist. *Other keywords:* winter, spring, fall. Also summer. *More keywords:* coffee, Yale School of Drama, zippers, age, lapsed Catholic, hiccups.

Jill Freedman

Jill's award-winning photography is included in the permanent collections of The Museum of Modern Art, the International Center of Photography, George Eastman House, the Smithsonian, and New York Public Library, among others. She has published seven books: *Old News: Resurrection City, Circus Days, Firehouse, Street Cops, A Time That Was: Irish Moments, Jill's Dogs,* and *Ireland Ever.*

David Frei

David is the longtime cohost of the annual Westminster Kennel Club Dog Show. He has appeared on *The Today Show, Good Morning America, The Early Show, Ellen, The View, Charlie Rose,* and many more. His book, *Angel on a Leash,* is a tribute to therapy dogs and the people who love them.

Beverly Gross

Beverly is a retired professor of English. She is currently painting and writing in New York City.

Linda Gross

Linda is a retired New York City psychologist, currently residing with her rescued Yorkshire Terrier, Archie, in Aventura, Florida. Following the unexpected loss of her brother, Garry, she has focused on ensuring the publication of this book, in recognition and remembrance of his life and work.

Elaine Hendrix

Elaine is a celebrated actress and creator of The Pet Matchmaker™, a multimedia resource for pet parents at any stage of pet parenting. Please visit www.elainehendrix.com and www.ThePetMatchmaker.com.

Jessica Jacobson

Jessica is a New York City native. After working as an equestrian instructor, apprenticing under Garry Gross, and dog walking, she founded Dapper Dog Training and now owns Dog Trainers of New York. She continues to use positive training methods and lives with her German Shepherd rescue, Minnie, in the West Village.

Leslie Jean-Bart

With a MA in journalism from Columbia University, Jean-Bart's photography career has taken him to Japan, Brazil, Iceland, Cyprus, and Portugal. His illustrations for the children's book *Strong to the Hoop* (Lee & Low Books) received the Marion Vannett Ridgway Memorial Award in 2000. His portraits have graced the covers of numerous national publications. Please visit www.lesliejean-bart.com.

Dean Koontz

Dean's books are published in thirty-eight languages and have sold over 400 million copies. Fourteen of his novels have risen to number one on the *New York Times* bestseller list. *Rolling Stone* has hailed him as "America's most popular suspense novelist." Dean lives with his wife, Gerda, and the enduring spirit of their Golden Retriever, Trixie, in Southern California.

Mara Kurtz

Mara is a graphic designer, photographer, and photo illustrator. Her work has won awards from the AIGA, Art Director's Club, and Graphis. Mara is a faculty member at Parsons School of Design, The New School, and School of Visual Arts. Her documentary photography book, *The Rock Hill Pictures* is available on Blurb.com.

Wendy Liebman

Comedian Wendy Liebman has been a regular on late-night television, including Carson, Fallon, Letterman, Kimmel, Ferguson, and Leno. Her Showtime special, *Wendy Liebman: Taller on TV* is available at www.wendyliebman.com.

Valerie Macys, Ph.D.

Valerie is the founder and president of Cocker Spaniel Adoption Center, Inc., a nonprofit organization that also rescues mixes and other breeds. CSAC even helps felines and wildlife. When she isn't rescuing, Dr. Macys is busy teaching English literature, writing her novel, or spending time with her own dogs—all rescues.

Carolyn Mason

Carolyn is a freelance writer living in Tuscaloosa, Alabama. She writes for trucking, landscaping, health/fitness, travel, and city magazines and covers anything to do with dogs. She is an adjunct instructor at the University of Alabama's Honor's College. E-mail: Carolynmason76@gmail.com.

Barbara Napoli

Barbara is the founder and owner of Critter Comfort pet sitting company. She lives with four Chihuahuas, five cats, one Pit Bull, two rabbits, two birds, and two turtles. "No other job has made me feel so satisfied, loved, and fulfilled. These animals have taught me how to live, and when my time comes, how to die with dignity."

John O'Hurley

John is best known for the role of J. Peterman on the NBC sitcom *Seinfeld* and was the host of the game show *Family Feud* from 2006 to 2010. He was a finalist on the first season of *Dancing with the Stars*. In 2011, John received the Ellis Island Medal of Honor for his commitment to humanitarian causes.

Eugene O'Neil

America's foremost dramatist and winner of the Nobel Prize for Literature in 1936, was born in New York in 1888 and died in Boston in 1953. His masterpiece, *Long Day's Journey into Night,* followed a long list of great plays, including *Beyond the Horizon* (1920), *Anna Christie* (1922), *Strange Interlude* (1928), *Ah, Wilderness!* (1933), and *The Iceman Cometh* (1946).

Ann Prival

Ann was born in New York City and went from kindergarten through psychoanalytic training free of charge because that used to be possible in NYC. For over twenty years, Ann was a psychoanalytic psychotherapist. Then she attended art school, worked for a picture archive, and then for an artists' copyright cooperative. Now, she does collage.

Anna Quindlen

Anna's Pulitzer Prize–winning work has appeared in America's most influential newspapers, many of its best-known magazines, and on both fiction and nonfiction bestseller lists. *Thinking Out Loud,* her collection of *New York Times* op-ed columns (1981 to 1994) was published by Random House. She has written four bestselling novels: *Object Lessons, One True Thing, Black and Blue,* and *Blessings.* With the release of *A Short Guide to a Happy Life* in 2000, Anna became the first writer ever to have books appear on the fiction, nonfiction, and self-help *New York Times* Best Seller lists. She holds numerous honorary doctorates and was awarded the University Medal of Excellence by Columbia. She was a Poynter Fellow in Journalism at Yale, a Victoria Fellow in Contemporary Issues at Rutgers, and a Fellow of the Academy of Arts & Sciences. *Glamour* magazine named her one of its 10 Outstanding Women of the Year. Quindlen is a graduate of Barnard College and lives with her family in New York City.

Laurie Rubin
Mezzo-soprano and recording artist Laurie Rubin has been praised by *The New York Times* for her "compelling artistry" and "communicative power." In addition to her concert and opera career, Rubin authored *Do You Dream in Color? Insights from a Girl without Sight* (Seven Stories Press 2012). She is cofounder of Ohana Arts in Hawaii.

Branka Ruzak
Branka is a writer, editor, and producer living in New York City. She is currently at work on a collection of essays about family, identity, and culture. Her essay "Hungry Heart" appears in *Dirt: The Quirks, Habits and Passions of Keeping House*, Seal Press, 2009.

Susan Seligson
Susan has written for, among others, *The New York Times Magazine, The Atlantic, The Boston Globe, Yankee,* and *Redbook*. She earned a master's in journalism at BU's College of Communication, is an award-winning humor columnist, and is the author of four books for children and two nonfiction books, including the travel memoir *Going with the Grain* (Simon & Schuster).

Ally Sheedy
Ally is an actor, writer, editor, teacher, and mom who lives in New York City.

Victoria Stilwell
Victoria, born and raised in England, is one of the world's most recognized and respected dog trainers. She is best known for her role as the star of Animal Planet's hit TV series *It's Me or the Dog,* which has now aired 110 episodes over eight seasons, reaching audiences in over fifty countries. Her two bestselling books, *It's Me or the Dog: How to Have the Perfect Pet* and *Fat Dog Slim: How to Have a Healthy, Happy Pet,* promote her core reward-based training philosophy: "There's a better way to train ... Positively."

Richard Storm
A native of Portland, Oregon, Richard moved to New York City to pursue an acting career. His first poetry collection, *Old Mr. Portland Official Poem-Readers Guide,* came out in 2011. His poems have appeared in *The New York Times, Möbius, The New Verse News,* and *First Literary Review-East.*

Julia Szabo
Julia has written about dogs for *The New York Post, The New York Times, The New Yorker, Dogster,* and *Cesar's Way,* among others. The author of *Animal House Style* and five other books, she's currently at work on a book about her dog's experience with adult stem cell regeneration therapy, and how that motivated her to seek the same high-tech treatment for herself. She lives in New York City with four rescued dogs: three Pit Bulls and a German Shepherd.

Marlo Thomas

Marlo is the author of six bestselling books, including *Free to Be ... You and Me, The Right Words at the Right Time,* and her memoir, *Growing Up Laughing: My Story and the Story of Funny.* The actress-activist has won four Emmy Awards, a Peabody, a Golden Globe, and a Grammy, and has been inducted into the Broadcasting Hall of Fame for her work in television, including her starring role in the landmark series *That Girl,* which she also conceived and produced. She is the National Outreach Director for St. Jude Children's Research Hospital, which was founded by her father, Danny Thomas, in 1962. She lives in New York with her husband, Phil Donahue.

Tanya and Toby Tobias

In 2001, Lucky adopted us. Ten years later, he inspired us to open Second Life, an upscale thrift store in Atlanta giving homeless pets a second chance at life. Our store sells gently used donated items and in turn, we give cash donations to animal rescue organizations. Lucky was sixteen and a half years old when he passed away in December 2011, but his legacy lives on. Please visit www.secondlifeatlanta.org.

Loudon Wainwright

Loudon Snowden Wainwright, the author of *Life* magazine's longtime column *The View from Here,* joined the staff of *Life* in 1949 as an office boy after serving in the Marine Corps. In 1964, Wainwright started *Life's* first personal column, which despite interruptions, he was still writing up until his death in 1988.

Lise Zumwalt

Lise works as a filmmaker in New York City and lives with her husband, Peter, her two children, Benny and Lucy, and her son-in-law, Waffle, who was adopted nine years ago and loves being part of the family. He is their first dog.

Acknowledgments

On behalf of everyone who knew Garry Gross—family, friends, colleagues, and neighbors—all those who loved, admired, respected, and cared for him, may I say thank you for these exquisite and highly memorable photographs and equally so, for the inspiring mission Garry has urged us to continue—calling attention to and caring for beautiful old dogs, wherever they may be.

We can love them so easily, feeling that empathy spot humming inside us because these dogs are like kids with special needs, especially the ones who don't express themselves in words. And when they get older and slower and the soul just deepens, we can't help loving them even more. This is what I have learned from doing this book.

I should thank Linda Gross, Garry's sister, for that gift. Linda first contacted me, asking that I find a way to actualize Garry's intentions and perpetuate his legacy. It's been my pleasure to become friends with Linda and realize her wishes.

Linda directed me to a number of Garry's friends and colleagues who have been helpful in putting this book together. Thanks especially to Victoria Stilwell, for writing the foreword, and to David Frei (and Bow Tie Press) for his own essay and for steering me to a number of other valuable contributors.

Thank you most kindly to everyone who contributed original stories, essays, and poems, as well as those who gave us permission to reprint previous works. Some had personal reasons for participating while others were happy to use their stories to promote the work they are doing helping senior dogs. In both cases, thank you for your time and generosity. Thanks especially to Richard Storm, David Lansbury, Charlotte Sheedy, and Gerit Quealy for their kind assistance.

A special thanks to Doris Day for supporting our book.

I know that Linda Gross joins me in expressing a deep gratitude to all those who contributed to the book and especially to James Schiavone, literary agent, and St. Martin's Press for making this book possible. Thanks specifically to Daniela Rapp at St. Martin's for her enthusiasm, keen eye, and gracious support. Thanks, too, to everyone else there for taking such good care of this project.

Finally, may I thank my children, Max and Stella, for keeping their paws on everything I do.

Permissions

"My Summer *(by Trixie Koontz, Dog)*" by Dean Koontz, from *A Big Little Life: A Memoir of a Joyful Dog Named Trixie* (Bantam Books 2009).

"Be Gentle: I Know My Dog Is Old" by Susan Seligson. This essay previously appeared in *The Bark*.

"The Big Blue Elephant" by John O'Hurley, from *Before Your Dog Can Eat Your Homework, First You Have to Do It: Life Lessons from a Wise Old Dog to a Young Boy* (Hudson Street Press 2007).

"Chasing Waves" by Carolyn Mason, adapted from *Old Man Doug: An Ode to Our 17-Year-Old Dog,* which first appeared on www.vetstreet.com.

"The Last Will and Testament of an Extremely Distinguished Dog" by Eugene O'Neill, published with permission from the Estate of Eugene O'Neill.

"Wisdom" by David Frei, from *Angel on a Leash: Therapy Dogs and the Lives They Touch* (Bow Tie Press 2011).

"A Cycle of Love" by Suzanne Clothier, from *Bones Would Rain from the Sky: Deepening Our Relationships with Dogs*. Copyright © Suzanne Clothier. By permission of Grand Central Publishing. All rights reserved.

"Chasing Fire Engines" by Jill Freedman, from *Jill's Dogs* (Pomegranate Artbooks 1993). Reprinted with permission from Jill Freedman.

"Another Sort of Love Story" by Loudon Wainwright, from *LIFE* magazine, January 22, 1971. Copyright © 1971. The Picture Collection Inc. Used with permission. All rights reserved.

"In Praise of Senior Dogs" by Tom Cushing. This is an excerpt from the original article that appeared in *The Bark*, Issue 63, Feb/Mar 2011.

"You Are the Man" by Anna Quindlen, from *Good Dog. Stay* (Random House 2007). Reprinted by permission.

Garry Gross
1937–2010